JACQUES ELLUL

M&ONEY POWER

Foreword by
David W. Gill

Translated by
LaVonne Neff

INTER-VARSITY PRESS
DOWNERS GROVE
ILLINOIS 60515

Originally published in 1954 as L'Homme et l'argent. *Second edition, enlarged,* © *1979 by Presses Bibliques Universitaires, Lausanne, Switzerland.*

English translation © *1984 by Inter-Varsity Christian Fellowship of the United States of America.*

All rights reserved. No part of this book may be reproduced in any form without written permission from InterVarsity Press, Downers Grove, Illinois.

InterVarsity Press is the book-publishing division of Inter-Varsity Christian Fellowship, a student movement active on campus at hundreds of universities, colleges and schools of nursing. For information about local and regional activities, write IVCF, 233 Langdon St., Madison, WI 53703.

Distributed in Canada through InterVarsity Press, 860 Denison St., Unit 3, Markham, Ontario L3R 4H1, Canada.

All biblical quotations unless otherwise noted, are from the Revised Standard Version of the Bible, copyrighted 1946, 1952, © *1971, 1973, and are used by permission.*

Cover illustration: Roberta Polfus

ISBN 0-87784-916-1

Printed in the United States of America

Library of Congress Cataloging in Publication Data

Ellul, Jacques.
    Money and power.

    Translation of: L'homme et l'argent.
    1. Wealth, Ethics of.   2. Money—Biblical teaching.
3. Money—Moral and ethical aspects.   I. Title.
HB835.E413   1984   261.8'5   83-22647
ISBN 0-87784-916-1

---

19 18 17 16 15 14 13 12 11 10 9 8 7 6 5 4 3
97 96 95 94 93 92 91 90 89 88 87

To my wife
who endures the problems of money with me

Foreword

Jacques Ellul, the recently retired professor of the history and sociology of institutions at the University of Bordeaux, has often said that he does not write on a purely theoretical or abstract level. His forty or so books emerge from serious reflection on life in this world, especially his own life and experience. This is as true of his best-known sociological studies —*The Technological Society, Propaganda* and *The Political Illusion*—as it is of the parallel stream of works he has produced as a lay theologian and Christian ethicist.

Just as Ellul's well-known study of *The Meaning of the City* grew out of his encounter as a modern urban man with the biblical message on the city, *Money and Power* is the result of wrestling with the problem of money in modern society in the context of the Genesis-to-Revelation message on wealth, poverty and money. Ellul has always argued that the one divine author behind the whole of Scripture has provided a unified revelation transcending or encompassing the diverse parts of the biblical canon. *Money and Power* attempts to discover this broad and unified biblical theology and ethics of money. As always in Ellul's biblical studies, the center of this revelation is Jesus Christ.

Ellul was born in 1912, the only child of a poor family in Bordeaux, a port city on the southwest coast of France. The economic crash of 1929 left his family with nothing and was, he says, his moment of discovery of real poverty. He worked from age sixteen onward to support himself and contribute to the family finances. Despite these financial obstacles Ellul was able to attend the University of Bordeaux, earning the Doctor of Laws degree in 1936. After just four years of teaching, he was dismissed from his post by the Vichy government when the Germans occupied France (1940-44). During the occupation Ellul worked with the French resistance and eked out an existence on a small farm outside of Bordeaux.

After the liberation in 1944, Ellul began his teaching career (which lasted until his retirement in 1980) at the University of Bordeaux and also served as Deputy Mayor of Bordeaux in charge of public works projects from 1944-46. Part of his reason for abandoning his political career in 1946 was the financial corruption of the city government. Since 1952 he has lived in a chateau near the university. Large but far from ostentatious, the Ellul home has been a meeting place for countless groups of people, including for many years a house church composed mostly of laborers and their families. Thus, after forty years of struggling with poverty, the Elluls have had to struggle with thirty or so years of relative financial security.

Money and Power was written and originally published in the early fifties, just as Ellul's personal fortunes were changing (along with those of many people in the West). At that time he and his wife were a young Christian family wrestling with what God has to say about wealth, poverty and money. As the 1979 Afterword indicates, Ellul believes his original analysis was on target. While he might be embarrassed for me to praise him too much, I must report that he has followed his own advice in not stockpiling savings over the years but rather "profaning" Mammon by giving money away to those in need. Those of us who have had the pleasure of knowing him have always been impressed by his integrity and humility in these matters. He practices what he teaches.

If we acknowledge Jesus Christ as Lord of the whole of life, then *Money and Power* addresses issues vital to our discipleship. We live in an affluent society. The media in general and the advertising industry in particular bombard us with messages to pursue money and material possessions as though they were gods. High-school and college vocational counselors urge us to choose our majors and our jobs primarily on the basis of the promise of financial success. The social activism of the sixties has been replaced by an aggressive materialism in the eighties. It is essential, then, that Christians allow the Word of God to challenge and remold their attitudes and behavior toward money and material things. This goes for all of us in all fields of study and work.

Money and Power has special relevance, however, for those in (or preparing for) careers in business, economics, finance and related fields. Christians in these fields must not allow their attitudes and policies to be shaped merely by the wisdom of this age, be it Milton Friedman, John Kenneth Galbraith, Adam Smith or anyone else. God has much to say about money and power: Christians in business must be shaped by this Word or forfeit all possibilities of being the salt of the earth and the light of the world.

Money and Power also constitutes an excellent model for what needs to be done in other fields. That is, lawyers and law students need to probe the very rich and full revelation of the Scripture on law and justice to illuminate their study and practice. Health-care specialists need to examine the biblical revelation on healing, disease and so on. *Money and Power* represents the kind of study that needs to be undertaken in all fields by Christians eager to be more faithful to their Lord.

In reading Ellul's work it is important to keep three things in mind. First, as indicated above, Ellul is writing out of his own experience in a French context. We need to rethink what he has to say within our own context and experience. Second, Ellul has never been one to place a high priority on systematic neatness and the resolution of all ambiguity. On the contrary, life is full of paradox and ambiguity, and the Bible itself displays various contrasts that can be very puzzling. Ellul's thought and style is thus very *dialectical:* it highlights the tensions and opposing forces within which God has placed us (for example, money is the god Mammon; money is merely a medium of exchange; wealth is associated with the curse; wealth is associated with the righteous Abraham). Ellul's point is that God will lead us faithfully through these paradoxes and difficulties, but we must recognize them for what they are and not collapse the tension into a simplistic little formula. Finally, Ellul does not offer *Money and Power* (or any of his other work) as the "final word." The only final word is Jesus Christ.

Ellul's purpose is to enlighten, but more than that to provoke in his readers a further exploration of the Word of God. *Money and Power* is nothing if it is not provocative and stimulating. Ellul shares his own thinking about wealth, poverty, the principalities and powers, savings, profaning money and so on, not merely to provoke further thought, but to incite action. *Money and Power* is intended to affect your life. "The course of history belongs to God, and if we as Christians have any influence on it, it is first of all by our faithfulness to his will" (p. 19).

David W. Gill
Associate Professor of Christian Ethics
New College Berkeley

CHAPTER ONE
THE PROBLEM OF MONEY: FROM THEORY TO REALITY

WHENEVER WE TALK ABOUT MONEY WE TEND TO LOOK AT IT through the eyes of the society in which we live. In our society, this means from the perspective of economic systems. Today we no longer see money as a substance to be hoarded, a treasure trove—once the only form of wealth. Money is a more complex idea. Money itself almost disappears into the related ideas either of legal tender or of economic wealth and power. Even if the term *money* is still used in everyday speech, it is rarely used by economists. And even in common parlance, *to have money* is more likely to mean "to have spending power" (that is, to earn and use income) than "to have a stash of precious metal"—once the only meaning of the phrase.

The Problem: Individual or Corporate?
We can no longer talk about money without thinking of the total econ-

omy. We are well aware that money is closely linked to all economic phenomena, that it affects each of the others. We also know that an individual cannot earn or spend money without becoming part of the complex interplay of the larger economy. In reality, money is nothing but the symbol of the total economy.

On the one hand, money, as the measure of the value, distribution or capitalization of wealth, has a definite economic function. But in a larger sense, money itself has no value beyond what the economy, according to its own prosperity, gives it. Over the last century money has been transformed; it has become abstract and impersonal.

Money has become *abstract* because the individual can no longer hold in his hands something that is valuable in itself; he can no longer attach a fixed meaning to the money he uses. Coins as well as paper money have become abstract symbols. The individual is attached not to his ten-dollar bill or ten-franc piece, but only to its buying power. The symbol itself, like the economic reality for which it stands, has become more abstract.

Money has become *impersonal* because it increasingly seems as if the use of money is not an individual act, does not signify personal control, but instead results from distant and complex interactions of which our acts are merely echoes. No longer is there any real relation between an individual and his money, because this money is abstract and impersonal. Consequently, moral problems concerning money no longer seem to exist.

Looking at money from a purely naturalistic viewpoint (which we must do if we want to understand the prevailing world view), we no longer seem responsible for our money, how we earn it or how we spend it, for in the impersonal interplay of the economy, we are quite insignificant.

Labor as well as management has this attitude. Misers no longer exist, for gold makes up only an infinitesimal part of the money supply. Gone as well are spendthrifts, thieves, the greedy. All these categories are irrelevant in the naturalist view.

Admittedly, a problem with money remains. But this problem is impersonal and abstract like money itself. All our individual attitudes depend on how this problem is solved. No need for any individual to make a decision, to question his or her own actions: money is simply a reality in one kind of economy. It is untouchable; the individual can do nothing about it. We each get our share of money. We spend it. What else can we do? If things do not go well, the most we can hope for is a change in the economy. And indeed, if money is an economic reality tightly linked to the social complex, what can we as individuals do when we see injustice, imbalance, disorder? In the presence of such an enormous machine, the individual act can hardly be taken seriously.

If we accept the abstraction and impersonality of money, ultimately there is only one question left to ask: How will this money be distributed? This is the only problem which seems worth considering because it is itself impersonal and abstract: individual acts will change almost nothing in this distribution. We therefore look for a system, whether capitalism, collectivism, socialism, communism, whatever. In any case, we look at the money question from its global perspective, and we try to solve the whole economic problem in order to solve, once and for all, the problem of money. From our present perspective, this procedure is perfectly normal and coherent.

Whenever we talk about money, we always end up by asking, How should we organize the economy?—or even, What economic system should I support? "At the moment," we explain, "I may not be using money the way I should, but when the new system (whatever it may be) is instituted, when the general money problem is solved, I in turn will become just."

Thus we subordinate moral and individual problems to the collective problem, to the total economic system. If a man is a thief, it is not his fault; his economic conditions were such that he could be nothing else. Let us beware. If we accept this excuse on behalf of a poor person, we must accept it for everyone. Both the capitalist who exploits workers and the farmer who dabbles in the black market are also involved in impersonal economic conditions which leave them no options. As soon as we accept the supremacy of global concerns and of the system, as soon as we agree that material conditions remove our freedom to choose, we absolve all individuals of all responsibility for their use of money.

Seen in this light, how can capitalism be more valid than communism, or communism than capitalism? The same error lies at the heart of both: the flight from responsibility and the pursuit of an alibi. When I want to talk about money, everyone hands me his system. "If there is a money problem, it is because the economic system is unsound." All we need to do to solve the money problem is to change the economic system. This amounts to predicting that man will become just and good, that he will know exactly what to do with his money, that he will no longer covet his neighbor's possessions, that he will no longer steal, that he will give up bribing women and public officials, that he will not be corrupted by his own material good fortune, that he will sympathize with the needy, that he will neither hoard his money nor waste it, that he will no longer dream of "upward mobility," that he will not use his accumulated wealth to gain power in society, that he will not use his money to humiliate others.

The Error of a Systemic Approach. Even if, by chance, such a state of affairs existed in the best of all possible economic systems, this system, unless it was a fearsome dictatorship, would be quickly corrupted. Trying to solve the problem of money through the total economic system is both an error and an act of cowardice. It is an error precisely because it refuses to consider the human element in the problem. It is posited on the strict neutrality of human nature, as if human passion and evil were not factors in the problem of money and would not always exist—as if capitalism or communism could be built in the abstract without taking human nature into account.

Undoubtedly Marx wanted to show that capitalism is intrinsically evil, that it leads impersonally and mechanically to human degradation, but when we study historical events and situations rather than yielding to our desire for system, we see that there is no fundamental reason for capitalism to turn to exploitation.

As theory, Adam Smith's idea of the harmony between private and public interests is perfectly valid. It requires us, however, to consider human nature in the abstract. If human nature is neutral (no need to require it to be *good*), then private and public interests agree. I accept that. But human nature is not neutral. And now, because people lust after money, capitalism is turning into a machine for oppressing, enslaving and hardening individuals. Today's big error is to think we must change capitalism, whether to return to a true free-market economy or to try socialism or communism.

Of course the slogan "To each according to his work"—then "To each according to his needs"—is every bit as admirable as Adam Smith's principle. There is no theoretical reason for it not to produce an excellent structure. (But after all, capitalism's goals also are admirable.) The problem is that, to the extent that human nature cannot be changed, this admirable structure will come to a miserable end because individuals will use it, not in high-minded scientific objectivity, but in a passionate pursuit of power.

I am well aware of Marxism's promise that moral life will change with economic circumstances. This hope is built on the presupposition that there is no such thing as human nature, but only a human condition. If individuals behave badly, it is because bad economic conditions. Nevertheless it must be recognized that this human condition is firmly anchored; it is made up of long-standing ancestral customs, and it will certainly not change in a few years. A very long time may be necessary to effect change. Now if we build a technically perfect system but leave people in their natural state, they will quickly spoil it, as they have spoiled capitalism. We must therefore enslave people, bind them with all possible political and psychological constraints—through police, work, propaganda, fear—to prevent them from giving free rein to their wicked lust for money which would derail the wonderful Marxist economic mechanism designed for the greatest good of humanity.

Who knows? If capitalism had used the same method, if it had created an enormous dictatorship in 1820, coercing people in every way, it might have succeeded in creating a stable system, giving to each according to his needs and eventually producing a satisfactory human nature.

For, as soon as such a dictatorship arises, we no longer know what is causing the change in human nature. Is it the economic system or the police state? Obviously the economy alone is not sufficient; the Russian experiment proves this. But in the end, it might be possible for a dictatorship—one that lasted for a very long time—to crush the human spirit completely.

Since the U.S.S.R. still has saboteurs, spies, deviants, the unpatriotic (all accused of acting for money), we must conclude that neither the power of the economic system nor that of the police force has thus far succeeded in extinguishing the lust for money or in subordinating the individual to money. But it is not unthinkable that after three, four, ten generations of totalitarianism, individuals may indeed be so crushed that they will have no more interest in money, no more passion of any sort; they will simply conform to the model society has set for them. We conclude that if the problem of money is eventually solved, it will have nothing to do with the excellence of the new economic regime; it will instead be a result of a dictatorship which finally breaks the human spirit.

A similar but quicker way to solve economic problems and the problem of money would be to kill everyone! In fact, the massacres required to maintain capitalism by means of wars or to establish communism by means of revolutions seem to point in this direction. In any case, any economic regime assumes the elimination of those who, by their need or lust for money, threaten to disturb the well-ordered economy.

Some of these, workers starved by the capitalist system, threaten disruption because they need money. They fight the system to get it and thus prevent the economy from functioning. So from time to time a war restores order. Others, kulaks betraying socialism, do not want to give up their money. They fight to keep their savings and their inheritances and thus block the establishment of communism. Others, profiteering public officials, use their position for personal gain, stealing from the people and from the state, thus preventing the fascist or Soviet plan from producing good results. So from time to time a bloody purge restores order.

But in all these cases it seems to be human nature (with its lust for money) that is corrupting the system. And that is why it is horribly wrong to believe that the problem of money can be solved by a system. It is horribly wrong thus to cheat man's hopes and thirst for virtue and honesty. "You want justice? Then establish my system." This is the error of all committed economists and others who think they can solve the problem without considering human nature.

The Hypocrisy and Cowardice of a Systemic Approach. But it is more than an error: it is also hypocrisy and cowardice. For then I ultimately ask no more than to believe the system-builder. It is so convenient. I don't have to think about what I do. I don't have to try to use my money better, to covet less, to quit stealing. It's not my fault. All I have to do is campaign for socialism or conservatism, and as soon as society's problems are solved, I will be just and virtuous—effortlessly. My money problem will take care of itself.

This attitude explains today's infatuation with economic systems. Young people of the middle class who are aware of their own injustice, whose consciences trouble them either because they have money or because they earn it rather easily at an undemanding job, do not dare examine their own use of money. They much prefer to join a party that works for social justice; they volunteer their time and even their money and take comfort in dreaming of the new society to which they are contributing. It is so much easier than struggling alone with the power of money. So easy and so reassuring.

And workers—consumed by hatred against their bosses or against the middle class because of their money, and ready to commit any sin to get this money—do not need to fight their hatred, their sin, their lust for money. They are justified by working for a system. Their hatred turns into passion for justice; their covetousness, into revolutionary spirit.

And capitalists or business executives who are forced by economic necessity to pay their workers low wages or to crush and ruin the competition, who have attained such professional objectivity that they can destroy their adversaries without even realizing it and without hating them (to the contrary, often with the best of will)—they too are justified by the system. Their use of money turns into a desire for freedom; their greed, into a legitimate vocation. Thus the system offers marvelous alibis to everyone. Personal money problems are a thing of the past: I don't need to worry about who I am or what I do because I support a system which answers for everything, is the key to all difficulties, and will solve for all humankind every problem that I come up against personally.

To solve the problem of money by joining a system is to choose an alibi which allows me, in all good conscience, to remain uncommitted. When I say this, I am not saying that those who belong to a party or union do nothing. I know full well their feverish activity, the number of meetings they organize, the tracts they distribute, the dues they pay, the inspections they make. But all this activity is a justification for avoiding personal decision making. *My* money? *My* work? *My* life? I don't have to worry about them because I am involved in such-and-such a movement which will take care of all that for everyone once it comes to power. This escape hatch gives me an enormously easy way to avoid facing reality and realizing the power money has over me. Enormously easy in spite of all the sacrifices, because this attitude allows me to believe, on the one hand, that personal money problems will solve themselves and, on the other, that my own attitude is righteous.

The first point is common to most political involvements: up till now, when personal, moral or spiritual problems came into people's lives, they had to face up to them; they had to choose, to decide, to discipline and control themselves, to acquire and manifest the "virtues." In the confrontation between man and money, whose seriousness is attested in the Bible and many other sources, each person was challenged to account for what he was. Now collectivistic involvement makes it unnecessary to face up to our own situation. It is not useful to solve our own problems or to control ourselves; the individual act is unimportant. We can rest assured that our public activity will solve our own moral and spiritual problems as well as those of other people. We are therefore free to give in to all our sins, our injustice, our lust for money: these things are minor if we have joined the comforting system. Its public activity gives us our hope, our sole guarantee and, at the same time, our justification.

For I am no longer just when I do good as an individual; by contrast, I am just (in my own eyes and those of my friends) when I have signed on the dotted line. I repeat, it matters little which system I join; they all have the same character. Thus I can continue to be extremely rich or to act like a scoundrel. If I have joined some social-justice system, both my money and my behavior are justified.

A remarkable fact that well illustrates the power of the system is that we usually turn the tables and condemn those who try to live according to personal standards. We call them hypocrites. This is the popular label for those who, dissatisfied with their lives, search for values that will bring about successful change. Such people may question, for instance, the worth of their money, the correctness of their own behavior, the consistency of their actions—although they are sometimes tripped up because they are not strong enough to make the necessary sacrifices and feel torn between ideals and practice. This is what those who the party-liners call hypocrites are like. Yet to modern eyes the attempt to wipe out personal problems by joining a system is not hypocritical!

Furthermore, those who evaluate these issues for themselves, who do not support collective action but find themselves individually confronting the powers of this world, are currently accused of doing nothing, of refusing action, of being uncommitted. Those who will not choose between capitalism and communism appear in the eyes of today's multitudes to have no interest in the problem of money. And everyone is persuaded that individual self-examination leads nowhere and cannot be serious.

We are looking here at a widespread attitude toward action and ethics. That which cannot be seen or counted does not exist. An action which cannot be expressed in numbers accomplishes nothing. Truth resides in the masses, and as long as the problem is not solved everywhere for everybody, nothing has been done (yet we have seen that it has no chance of ever being solved everywhere). It is therefore strange that activists who do not even see the problem can accuse of being uninvolved those who, in desperation, stay at the very heart of the question. It is strange that those who sacrifice everything except their souls can accuse of being amateurs those who lay even their souls on the table. It is strange that those who attack an adversary whom they know only hazily can accuse of being ineffective those who try to understand, to diagnose and to strategize before acting.

Undoubtedly we must continue to criticize those who try to solve personal problems while refusing to look at their social context, or who try to find solutions without regard to social consequences. We know that the process of research tempts some people to do nothing, and we know that a person who is forever asking major questions and staking his life on them often remains passive. Nevertheless, there is an inactivity that is honest, and it is likewise uncomfortable. The reason for this inactivity is the extreme difficulty of incarnating truth. But this position is worth more than the absurd activism which plunges blindly ahead, bringing about results just the opposite of what it intends (because of lack of knowledge and understanding), randomly enlisting lives in the service of unfounded and valueless goals. This position is worth more than the search for an alibi which characterizes involvement in a system.

Of course individual attitudes cannot solve general problems, and capitalism will not be transformed by individual action. We have no recipe for global situations. But it is far from certain that collective action, whether political or economic, would do any better. Only a blind and absurd optimism would allow anyone to say today that socialism will solve all the economic and financial problems of capitalism or that a return to the free-market economy with the restriction of governmental powers will suffice to purify the land.

In any case, we must choose according to some scale of values. We judge that a collective solution to the global economic problem is of primary importance—a coherent materialist position. Or we judge that individual decisions made in the presence of God have priority. Our decisions may have far-reaching consequences, sooner or later transforming the whole environment, but we have no certain guarantee. The course of history belongs to God, and if we as Christians have any influence on it, it is first of all by our faithfulness to his will. Everything that tends to turn us away from this faithfulness (first expressed as recognition of sin, then as acceptance of grace, finally as personal commitment to personal action) diminishes Christian effectiveness, even if outwardly we do a great deal, changing institutions and mobilizing the masses.

Capitalism, Socialism and Christianity
I do not mean that we must reject all collective action and all quests for more workable social theories. But this must be secondary and, in any case, should take place only *after* we have come to understand the spiritual reality of forces or of institutions. This also means *after* we have individually confronted the problem that originally triggered our involvement. Now with respect to money, we can easily measure the impotence of all present systems. We cannot analyze them in depth here.

But we must observe that the two principal protagonists agree on one thing: that capitalism is the economic and social structure which has put the use of money in first place.

Capitalism. Beginning in the Middle Ages when money had very little importance and played only a minor role in human life, thought and concern, capitalism has progressively subordinated all of life—individual and collective—to money.

Money has become the criterion for judging man and his activity. One by one the state, the legal system, art and the churches have submitted to the power of money. This is the rule, not the exception, and it has nothing to do with corruption. As a matter of fact everyone has begun to think that money, the source of power and freedom, must take priority over everything else. This belief is well supported on the one hand by a general loss of spiritual sensitivity (if not of faith itself) and on the other by the incredible growth of technology.

Looking at the material success that money has allowed us to achieve, how could anyone deny the excellence of money, the source of progress? Money, which allows us to obtain everything material progress offers (in truth, everything our fallen nature desires), is no longer merely an economic value. It has become a moral value and an ethical standard.

We must recognize the truth in Karl Marx's observation that money, in the capitalist system, leads to alienation. One of the results of capitalism that we see developing throughout the nineteenth century is the subservience of *being* to *having*. This result makes allegiance to capitalism virtually impossible for a Christian. For it is not a by-product, something that might not have happened, a result that could be eliminated by a better organization of capitalism. To the contrary, it is the inevitable consequence of capitalism, for there is no other possibility when making money becomes the purpose of life.

The work ethic (that work is virtuous because it produces money) obviously leads to the subordination of being to having. Any other possibility would require us to dethrone money, give economic activity a smaller role, put the brakes on technological progress, and bring personal and spiritual life to the forefront—in other words, to destroy capitalism. But if we did all these things, money would no longer cause global, collective or social problems. It would no longer be necessary to take sides on economic theory or to join a system.

Socialism. Does socialism, then, look more attractive? Socialism rightly attacks capitalism for subordinating man to money, for its unjust economic structures. Socialism takes for its motto "To each according to his work," which in communism becomes "To each according to his needs."

This is all well and good. But how does socialism plan to achieve its goals? First, by strictly limiting human life to work, to economic activity. Everything else is superfluous, a superstructure made to give pleasure and happiness. Serious things have to do with work and production. It is even appropriate for people to work harder than ever before, because the future of socialism is tied to intense production.

Of course we are positing honest socialist structures with a just distribution of goods and no unfair stockpiling. But even in such an ideal case we have organized life and society around the supremacy of the economic system. Individuals are still subordinated to their work, which itself is mandated by the needs of the world community. It is possible to say, without paradox, that socialism takes the worst features of capitalism and carries them to extremes while justifying them theoretically. In socialist society individuals are doubtless freed from subordination to others, such as capitalists, but they remain entirely submitted to production: the economy is the basis of their lives. This is precisely the source of real alienation—not the subservience of *being* to *personal having,* but the subservience of *being* to *doing* and to *collective having*.

The differences between systems look small next to such similarity. Socialism forcefully affirms the supremacy of economic activity over all other activity. Moreover, this error is so deeply rooted in long-standing customs and possesses such a weight of evidence that it passes for truth in the eyes of most. It turns socialism into a product of the very evil demonstrated by capitalism in its degenerate state.

Someone may agree with my argument so far but observe that it has little to do with money. In any case, the role of money in capitalism is very different from its role in socialism. In socialism money, by itself, cannot be a means of possessing and oppressing man. True enough. In socialism money is not the motivator of all economic activity. This motivator is the state.

But in closely examining the situation, we see that the role of money is not so different after all. Money has the practical function of measuring value, circulation and capitalization. Although capitalization is not done by individuals, it still exists. Money is no longer one person's instrument of power. Such is progress. It would be major progress if socialist reality corresponded with its theory. But the relation between man and money, like the general function of money in the economy, remains the same in socialism as in capitalism. For it matters little that the form of money is changed—whether a bill represents the state gold supply (no longer the case even in capitalist countries) or national assets or national labor, as in Hitler's Germany, whether a bill represents a stated amount of work entitling its holder to a stated amount of merchandise or, at the far extreme of socialism, whether it is a ticket representing specific merchandise available without charge—it all amounts to the same thing with respect to human problems.

These are only outward variations corresponding to one organizational type or another; basically the situations are the same and the reality of money is similar. We are well aware, for example, that ration coupons gave rise to exactly the same relations, passions, exchanges and powers as money. The coupons took on the value of money. The reality of money, symbol of economic power, is not about to disappear—and this fact strengthens the economy.

Ultimately socialism does not resolve the money problem any more than does capitalism. In some ways it may appear more just; in others, more oppressive; in any event it is neither the kind of total liberation nor the suppression of the dangerous man-money relationship that it is made out to be. No economic system can settle this question. No economy can function without money; to think it possible is pure utopianism. Only abstract, impractical schemes give such an illusion. Insofar as the economy (free-market or planned) is real, we see that it is linked with money, for money is nothing but the expression of economic life.

But any system which would provide a balanced economy is threatened by our own lack of balance; the system, rather than solving the man-money problem, risks being annihilated by it. We therefore cannot escape the necessity for personal decision making that we would prefer to avoid at all costs. We want to avoid it because it introduces personal risk into our life and because, faced with the enormity of the task, we see no way to provide a global solution for this individual problem. For it goes without saying that in our eyes nothing is accomplished without a solution that is global and general.

It is true that we are catching a glimpse today of one possible solution: crushing human beings with propaganda, thus integrating them completely into the system. This would eliminate the individual's problem with respect to money, simply by eliminating truly human beings themselves, leaving only psychological mechanisms in their place. Only by annihilating individual conscience can the system regulate both the objective organization of society and human passion, which from the beginning has both used and bowed down to the power of money.

A Christian Approach. Now as Christians we absolutely cannot accept this solution and start down this path. We have already observed, to be sure, that the supremacy (both spiritual and rational) of the individual over the system need not stop certain Christians from looking for objective solutions. But we must bear in mind that Christians are not required to do this, and that in any case this is not true commitment. To believe that joining a movement is the same as committing oneself is simply to capitulate to today's sociological trends, and it is to follow the herd while claiming to make free choices. Better to judge the herd instinct beforehand and give in to it only when it is objectively valid, as we are trying to do here; otherwise we are in exactly the situation described by St. Paul: "children, tossed to and fro and carried about with every wind of doctrine" (Eph 4:14). It is painful to see countless Christians in this situation.

Among the three or four major systems trying to apply an organization to money, do we have to choose? And which should we choose? In fact, neither theology nor Scripture gives us any criteria for evaluating one system against another. Since no economic mechanism corresponds to Christian truth, if we wish to choose we will have to do so for purely natural reasons, knowing that our choice will in no way express our Christian faith. If we like these superficial involvements, if we want to work with other people in group endeavors, nothing in the Christian faith prevents our choosing conservatism or cooperativism or socialism, provided that we retain our sense of the relative along with a healthy skepticism for these inadequate recipes—and provided above all that we not regard our activity as a direct and natural outgrowth of the Christian faith. It is understandably disappointing not to have a system corresponding in all points to Christian faith and doctrine. But beware: the disappointment is not in Christianity but in the system. Christianity is infinitely too realistic, and revelation shows us far too clearly what man and the world really are, for us to be able to base a system on it. For no system can either correspond to this reality or organize it. Certainly no system in the world allows us to reduce Christianity to its political or economic aspects, and this becomes even more obvious when we look at actual situations. It is indeed possible to maintain illusions so long as we are looking only at great principles and broad ideas. A given system may, from the standpoint of its philosophy or intentions, seem to conform to Christian ideas. But we should already be on guard because there are not many *ideas* in Christianity: faith and knowledge are based on real events and situations that are closely related to man; they have nothing to do with ideas, principles, and so forth.

Now it happens that when we examine any economic system in detail, we find more and more discord. While from a general point of view a particular system may look valid to a Christian, if we look at what Scripture clearly tells us about economic questions, we realize that the system is neither a solution from the human standpoint nor an answer to the question God asks us in Scripture. The same thing happens when we look at money itself. None of the major systems has anything reasonable to say once we are aware of what money really is in the light of Scripture.

But then, we think, could not Christianity itself propose a global solution, an economic doctrine of its own? Most Christians who have studied this topic have concluded that no Christian political doctrine exists; it cannot be constructed either from biblical texts or as a logical outworking of Christian principles.

It is not possible to speak of a Christian doctrine of money, first because that is not why we have been given revelation through the Scriptures, and it is even less why Jesus was born, died and was raised from the dead. The purpose of Christianity is not to provide useful rules for living or organizational schemes. From the perspective of salvation, how the world is organized is not of major importance. Of course it is fine for human beings to organize the world, but this is a *fallen* world and redemption is not tied to our organization of it. Consequently God's work, which is from the beginning the work of redemption, cannot in any detail be expressed by social, economic or other worldly organization. We cannot extract any system from God's revelation without twisting the texts and coming up with unwarranted conclusions because redemption is not a system.

No doubt the problem of money is very important, but we cannot build a system on that basis. This is so, and this is the second reason we cannot speak of a Christian doctrine of money, because no objective solution exists. When we open the Bible we do not find a philosophy, a political statement, a metaphysic or even a religion. We find instead the promise of dialog, a personal word addressed to me, asking me what I am doing, hoping, fearing—and especially what I am.

All that the Bible has to tell me about money is found in this dialog. It offers no objective discovery on which to base a general system. It instead offers truth about all things—including money. But it leads us to this dramatic conclusion: truth is not objective (nor is it subjective!). It is found in relationship with God, and nowhere else. Thus a person who has received truth can make it known only in making known this relationship with God. It is perfectly useless to try to extract from the Bible a money system applicable to the world because people will recognize the truth only after they have come to faith. The immense body of revelation—which contains, among other things, wisdom about money—does not appeal to reason, evidence or pragmatism; indeed, it is shut tight against these modes of conviction.

When looking at biblical passages about money, then, we must let them have the character God has given them. First, these are fragments of the total revelation, and we have no right to detach them from the whole in order to consider them separately, objectively. They are there because their content refers to God's work in Jesus Christ; we cannot pull them out of this context.

Second, these passages have to do with the relation between God and man (this is the context for biblical statements about money), and we have no right to turn them into simple descriptions of the relation between man and money. They are based on the personal relationship that is fundamental to the whole work of salvation; therefore we cannot abstract them from a general idea, applicable to the world.

Third, these texts ask us to commit ourselves. They start us down a certain path. They are not providing us with rational options or objective conclusions; the biblical texts never come to conclusions because there is no conclusion apart from the heavenly Jerusalem and our resurrection. The texts are therefore never a "solution." To the contrary, they get us started on a journey, and the only answer we can hope to find is the one we ourselves give by our lives as we proceed on that journey. This absence of systematic conclusions destroys every attempt to base an ideological or ethical system on Scripture. We must resign ourselves to this. And if we will not accept it, we are so refusing biblical truth that if we ever did find a Christian financial or economic or political system and happened to accept it, we would be basing our acceptance on its non-Christian features! This would be a tragic mistake.

Traditional and Recent Christian Responses
Now in its approach to the reality hidden by all doctrinaire systems (and, to a great extent, by economic theory itself), the Bible does not speak to us about human nature only. It speaks about human beings in this world—human beings in relation to things, organizations, economic and political forces. It speaks to us about these things realistically (we shall look further at this realism later). And everything the Bible says to us about money or wealth is stamped with this hard realism. It is here and not in some idealized society that God calls us to live. *To live* means in part "to exist," but it also means "to fulfill an individual calling or a collective destiny."

In this implacable society where the state uses its power to oppress and money uses its power to possess, God in Jesus Christ calls the Christian to live according to God's will; in other words, to accomplish something truly extraordinary.

God never proposes that people collectively should turn society into an earthly paradise, only that individuals, called to very specific tasks, fulfill his purposes in this environment and not some other.

The church has interpreted this order two ways. A major current, including medieval Christianity, the Byzantine Church and to a certain extent the Orthodox Church, has identified society with the church. This identity we call Christendom. All members of society are expected to act like Christians. Economic structures and the use of money, for instance, must not be based on the law of the world but on church law; the whole society must submit to the Christian order. Such society is no longer that which the Bible describes, for Scripture speaks only of a pagan world. Now times have changed, and if we do not impose Christ's law on everybody, we are being disorderly and disobedient.

Unfortunately this wish to sanctify society leads to disaster, to a denial of the very foundations of Christianity, to the triumph of law over grace. It cannot be otherwise. For the Bible's diagnosis does not change: as long as fallen creation exists, the world will be the world and money will be money. In the church's great battle against money during the Middle Ages (prohibition of interest, exaltation of poverty, regulation of commerce, just-price and fair-wage theories, organized philanthropy, etc.), the church was defeated because it thought it was possible to Christianize and make morally acceptable what will always be the indomitable adversary. The church was also defeated because it gave up its true weapons, accepting someone else's victory as its own, a victory which will never be definitive in the eyes of the world.

The other interpretation, coming from Lutheranism, consists in withdrawing from the world. Christianity has no business there. Let the world follow its course according to the law of the Fall and of gravity, under the rulership of perverts and cynics; the words of the Bible apply only to an infinitesimal fraction of humanity, Christians, and only to their inner lives. There is therefore a religious domain and a secular domain. In the latter, the Christian can do nothing.

This idea, as we have sketched it, abandons a fundamental theme of revelation: the Incarnation.

The world, following its own law without any Christian presence, becomes worse than ever before. Lacking the continuing presence of the Word of God, as it is preached and as it is lived, the world is set adrift. We have observed this ever since the Reformation.

And Christians are called to live in this unanchored world, to use money, for example, and to use it just like everyone else—according to money's own laws. But they of course try to justify their position, which seems to be no more than personal preference. They try to build some bridge between faith and social behavior. The more effective their social behavior, the more pressured they are to do this. If Christians prove to be honest business executives, active and serious, clever in their virtue and pragmatic in their morality—successes—they must find a way to justify their success.

Money as Blessing. Thus they bring God into the picture, and we find two views of money (among many others) which are especially prevalent among Protestants. The first view comes from the idea that money is God's blessing. To a great extent, as we shall see, this is true. But Christians have turned this blessing into a proof. They have turned it into a mathematical equation: money = blessing. No longer does a person receive money—more than is needed, superfluous abundance given by God—as a result of being blessed. Money becomes in itself a spiritual value.

If it is true that all blessing includes material success (and therefore money), can we not say that all accumulated wealth, all fortune, is the fruit of a blessing? If we do, we give ourselves a remarkable way to assure ourselves of this uncertain blessing! If we are never entirely sure of being blessed, if some last question always remains to haunt us, it is easy enough to find our assurance in money! That at least can be counted and measured. And as long as we have money, we can be assured that we also have grace.

It is therefore imperative that we make money. And this is where we end up because it is so important to us to be assured of blessing. "Get rich," says a proponent of this doctrine to young Christians who ask him what they should be doing. All activity then is directed toward acquiring money, evidence of the spiritual victory which automatically accompanies it.

I am not exaggerating. This deviation lies at the root of the attitudes of many American Christians among others. I will try to point out the correct relationship, as depicted in Scripture, between money and blessing. I hardly need to point out all the possible heresies found in the attitude described above: the wish to be assured of blessing, the strict equation of two terms which should be at God's free disposal, equating success with God and with the world, wishing to justify oneself. I need not press the point.

The Dangers of Stewardship. More subtle, and today more widespread, is the notion of *stewardship*. It is a Calvinist and Neo-Calvinist idea. Men and women are stewards chosen by God to manage the earth. It follows that the rich, who have many opportunities in this area, must both share these opportunities with others and give an account to God for their administration. Here again the starting assumptions are not completely incorrect, even though we again find the error of separating several texts from their context. We forget too easily that if man is God's steward according to the texts in Genesis, this is true primarily in the order of creation—and we abuse the text by extending that which belongs to the order of creation to the order in which we now live, the order of the Fall. We forget too easily that a rather important event lies between these two orders.

Moreover, if it is true in the faith that we must recognize that we get our possessions from God and must manage them for him, this does not apply at all outside the faith. In reality men and women get wealth unfairly; they willingly strip God of it and appropriate it to themselves; they are *not* stewards. They are unfaithful trustees, and they take care of Satan's wealth. It is idealistic to wish to extend to all humankind a situation limited to conscious Christians.

And further, even with Christians the idea of stewardship leads to concrete results which are far from beneficial in practice. Supporters of this idea have carried into their business life the conviction that they have been chosen by God from among all other people to direct the affairs of the world and to bring about the common good. This naturally leads to a conception of leadership by divine right and a kind of paternalism. Other people must be put under our guardianship, because in God's plan they can attain worldly goods only through us. Obviously God chooses the most capable to be his stewards. The rest must benefit from their administration without participating in it.

We must certainly see to their material happiness, but we must also put them to work. The management of worldly goods requires work from everyone—and if we have an account to give to God, it will be about our use and fair distribution of the world's wealth. But in everything we are the superiors, and nowhere do we give any sign of wishing to give others their freedom in God. This whole position is brilliantly criticized in one brief sentence: "It forgets that God's possessions belong to Jesus Christ, and in him to our neighbor, the one who is deprived of what we own" (Mlle. Moussat, Bulletin *Jeune Femme,* July 1952). After that incisive refutation, in which every word has meaning, it is unnecessary to present long arguments. The idea of stewardship is a useful reminder that we do not own our belongings and that we will have an account to give, but it becomes downright vicious when we use it to justify ourselves, when it permits us to fix in concrete what God wants us to submit to the Holy Spirit.

Ultimately all attempts to create a Christian economic doctrine run into this: we perpetually try to settle definitions, arguments, terms, to come up with a final construction that, intellectually and economically, we can rely on and trust. But the theme of Scripture is exactly the opposite—it concerns a movement. What Scripture shows has the strength and speed of a rushing torrent. We do not build with a torrent. At most, we can make it disappear into water pipes. That is exactly what we do when we insert the Word into our systems. And if we leave it free, it is like a dazzling rush down toward man and up toward God; it is like the beam of light from a projector that leaves great areas of darkness in order to focus on the one indispensable point where God's action is concentrated. This beam of light follows everything in a constant movement toward its death and its re-creation. In this movement there is no doctrinal stabilization, not even dialectical. And we understand that objective solutions to the problem of money, like subjective ones, are thrown out of court. They are equally useless and inadequate.

For the Spirit blows where he wishes . . .

Today's Challenge

Today we may be witnessing the dawn of a third attempt by Christians to address the problem of money. The first two ended in defeat, a victory for the world, a loss of certain fundamentals of Christian life and truth. The church can no longer attempt either to manage the world of money or to content itself with leaving money matters to the individual.

All that the church has been able to say about the exclusively personal nature of our use of money is no doubt true, but it is obsolete because of the character of the world in which we live. The church can neither vaguely repeat its ideas about the usurer or the good boss nor deny the form currently taken by the powers of money.

The church must not adapt to the world. Quite the opposite, it must rediscover the truth that has been revealed to it, the truth of Incarnation. The world itself once again seems to be God's instrument in forcing the church to face up to its conscience.

The church must no longer preach to the inner man alone but to the whole man, recognizing the personal element in the structures of the twentieth-century world. And if the church, for example, challenges all accepted positions about the reality of money because the truth of these matters has been revealed to the church alone, it should not then take refuge in a new abstraction which has nothing to do with humanity today or with the structures of our times.

We are invited to make a voyage of discovery. But we still must start from assured bases. It seems as if the church has lost sight, in the course of its experience, of the foundations which are both permanent and contemporary. I am here trying to remind us of these foundations, because wisdom for today is already inscribed in them. The church is like "a householder who brings out of his treasure what is new and what is old" (Mt 13:52).

CHAPTER TWO
WEALTH IN THE OLD TESTAMENT

MONEY AND WEALTH SYMBOLIZE CONTRADICTION NOT ONLY IN secular life, but also in the church and even in Scripture, which is revealed by God. And this should make us all the more aware of God's power. We should not be disturbed that the Bible contains contradictory texts about wealth, for it contains opposing texts on almost every subject. We well know that these contradictions are usually only apparent, for the unity of the Spirit is powerfully revealed.

But with wealth the situation is somewhat different. We find ourselves confronting conflicting trains of thought, and we can point to at least two discrepancies. The first is between the New Testament and the Old. Incontestably, in the New Testament wealth is condemned. To my knowledge there is not one text that justifies it. The Old Testament, on the other hand, presents wealth as a blessing, willed by God and pleasing to him. There is no more apparent radical opposition between the two covenants than the one concerning wealth. The second discrepancy is found within the Old Testament itself, between its judgment on the wealthy and its judgment on wealth. The conflict is unique: whereas, as we just said, wealth is considered good and just in the Old Testament, the wealthy are almost always judged and condemned.[1] This, obviously, is surprising, for if abundant possessions are God's gift to the righteous, how can the Old Testament so forcefully attack those who enjoy this abundance? Of course, we must remember that the wealthy are those who have a great deal not only of money but also of all other human strengths such as intelligence, integrity and family. We must also note that the Old Testament speaks of rich men who are also righteous and who are examples of righteousness, but their righteousness is neither moral virtue nor a particular way of using their wealth. On the contrary, according to the general teaching of the Old Testament, it is their righteousness that gives meaning to their wealth.

Righteous Rich Men

We meet three models of rich men who are righteous: Abraham, Job and

---

[1]To resolve this conflict, historians have noted that the texts condemning the wealthy are almost all taken from the prophetic books. Consequently they reason that this condemnation does not express the general thought of the Old Testament, but only the prophetic viewpoint. Other viewpoints (such as wealth as blessing) come from other times or places. This argument is not compelling. It is true that texts favoring wealth are usually in the Pentateuch and that texts condemning it are usually in the Prophets. But we cannot use this information to make a case for historical development, for (1) either the Pentateuch in its present form is earlier than the prophets (which historians do not admit), but then the favorable attitude toward wealth is inconsistent with the social and political state of the ninth century; or (2) the Pentateuch comes after the Prophets (as is generally held), but that raises two difficulties: (1) from a moral standpoint, the Pentateuch would then represent a regression from the prophetic message, yet (b) still later books like Ecclesiastes once again take up the condemnation of wealth.

It is useless to try to separate the prophetic from the priestly position. This division, which at first seemed to explain all discrepancies, is contested more and more by modern historians, and the hypothesis does not look like it will last much longer. The only wise attitude is to assume that we are looking at a unity composed of apparently contradictory terms. These contradictions will be resolved, however, not by a historical or sociological cleavage, but by a thorough analysis of the meaning of the texts and a rediscovery of the spiritual reality behind the social mask. Besides, we must be careful not to overstate the case: there are texts condemning the wealthy in the Pentateuch!

Solomon. To understand what wealth represents we must see how the righteousness of these men operates with respect to their wealth.

Abraham. Abraham had many possessions. When he heard the Lord's call, he left his city, Ur, where we can suppose his fortune was located. He left everything behind him; he followed God's order to leave. It would not be correct, however, to think only of his renunciation of wealth. This was his first action. But as soon as he heard God's word addressed to him (in other words, as soon as he was justified), Abraham repudiated his social position and his security; then, when he left his native land, he repudiated his wealth. God, in his revelation, put himself between this man and his possessions.

The theory that Abraham was a rootless nomad in the vicinity of Ur, whose wealth was nothing but flocks of sheep, waters down the story without explaining anything. It is better to stick with the concise information in the text. Moreover, Abraham takes with him as much of his wealth as he can, especially flocks and servants, silver and gold. But Abraham's detachment from his wealth is complete. He will not allow wealth to cause conflict among his people. He separates from Lot in order to avoid strife, leaving his nephew free to choose the best land. Against the natural law which would give him precedence, he gives Lot first choice. He subordinates himself without paying attention to his own need to find pasture for his flocks. In actual fact, Lot takes the richest land, and Abraham puts up with the desert and the mountains.

And as he renounces wealth Abraham receives God's promise concerning this land. Because he gave up his right of first choice and the foundation of his fortune, Abraham is given the whole land. "All the land which you see I will give to you and to your descendants for ever" (Gen 13:15). This wealth is not only material. Neither is it actual. It is a promise, but it is *God's* promise. And from this time forth what characterizes Abraham is that he actually (and not only in words) obtains his wealth from God. He refuses to receive it from anyone else. The meeting between Abraham and the king of Sodom is vital in that connection.

After Abraham's victory over Chedarlaomer, who had plundered Sodom and Gomorrah, all this wealth is in Abraham's hands. The king of Sodom gives it to him.

"The king of Sodom said to Abram: 'Give me the persons, but take the goods for yourself'" (Gen 14:21). Abraham answered the king of Sodom: "I have sworn to the LORD God Most High, maker of heaven and earth, that I would not take a thread or a sandal-thong or anything that is yours, lest you should say, 'I have made Abram rich.' I will take nothing but what the young men have eaten, and the share of the men who went with me; let Aner, Eshcol, and Mamre take their share'" (Gen 14:22-24).

In Abraham's refusal, we see first his concern not to depend on man for wealth. The way he formulates his refusal shows that he is not acting for merely political reasons, as we too easily conclude; he does not refuse because he is afraid this gift will ally him with the king of Sodom, but because of the Lord. Because the Lord is master of heaven and earth, Abraham can accept nothing from anyone else. To receive wealth from someone else is to deny God's lordship. To try to make money by whatever means possible, to give it first place in one's affections, to extract it from work or from war, is not to recognize this lordship, which cannot be simply a comforting word but must be an attested reality.

Further, Abraham shows here that, as God's representative and having acted with his strength, he must not lay himself open to what this pagan king of Sodom might say or think. This king must not be able to say, "I have made Abraham rich." Only God can say, "I have made Abraham rich." The first explanation of Abraham's refusal, his recognition of God's lordship, is for all humankind. The second explanation, his consideration of the effect his acceptance would have on others, focuses on the church. This word from the father of believers weighs heavily on the church, which has no right to receive wealth from pagan powers, especially gifts from non-Christian millionaires, charitable though they may be. This also applies to state subsidies. When the church accepts this money, even for good causes, it gives the powers of this world an unimaginable hold over it. And even if these powers are entirely impartial, it gives a counterwitness by allowing a person or the government to say, "I have made the church rich." The church thus becomes part of the world, letting the door close that it ought always to keep open.

Job. Abraham's attitude shows how he can be both rich and righteous. We see the same sort of righteousness in Job. Right from the beginning we see that wealth is a temptation. Satan says to God, "Job is just, upright, a man of integrity because he is rich, because you have blessed him." We often hear this idea from the poor, the unfortunate, laborers, employees, small businessmen: "Honesty and piety and justice are luxuries. When you have what you need to live well, then you can also afford to be religious and moral; but when you're poor, you don't have time for such frills." Job's prologue (written at a time when middle-class morality did not exist, but wealth did) shows us that this popular attitude is a word from Satan, and those who promote it are Satan's mouthpiece.

Of course, Satan adds, "If you take away his wealth, Job will stop being righteous." The whole problem is a love problem. What or who does Job love? Wealth or God? We already see that we can love only one or the other, that reconciliation of the two is impossible. Job loses his wealth. He has nothing left. And he suffers a violent depression. He rips his coat; he shaves his head. God never forbids us to have human emotions. If Job collapses after losing his wealth and his family, God does not reproach him.

But to whom is Job really attached? Will he sink in despair, will he accuse God of being unjust? That is the big question. Is God just when he favors us, makes us rich and blesses us? Is he unjust when he punishes, takes away our possessions and condemns us? Does God have an account to keep with us? Will we accept his judgments only if we understand them?

Job does not understand, but Job knows that all he had was really God's, that God can do as he pleases, that he gives and takes away according to his will, and that what counts is communion with him and not the things he gives us for a little while. Job loves God more than God's gifts, and he will not depart from God simply because God takes away everything that made life happy, good and blessed. "Naked I came from my mother's womb, and naked shall I return; the LORD gave, and the LORD has taken away; blessed be the name of the LORD" (Job 1:21). What is true of material wealth is also true of spiritual wealth.

When his wealth disappeared, Job did not abandon him who is his righteousness. He did not depend on his wealth as he depended on God who was his whole life. But note that both Abraham and Job went beyond mere words. It was not enough for them to say, "Naturally, we love God more than our money." They had to prove it. Zechariah even tells us that it is terribly dangerous to say, "Blessed be the LORD, I have become rich" (Zech 11:5). It is not enough to bless the Lord when one is rich; in fact, this brings God's wrath, as the rest of the passage shows. Every declaration that has never been put to the test is suspect: God asks Job and Abraham for concrete evidence.

Solomon. The righteousness of Solomon in his wealth is entirely different from that of Job and Abraham. Right at the beginning God makes Solomon choose: "Ask what I shall give you" (1 Kings 3:5). Solomon knows his role: he is David's successor and must bring his political work to its peak; he is the king chosen by God to build the Temple. Solomon knows that to do this he will need much strength and much wealth. It would be legitimate (not for himself but for this work willed and planned by God) to ask God for the tools needed to accomplish it. It would be legitimate to ask for wealth and power because these would serve God's purposes. But no, it is not legitimate. Solomon asks (verse 9) for "an understanding mind to govern thy people, that I may discern between good and evil" (*to govern* means to convey God's word to them).

These two aims of wisdom show that Solomon is requesting the Holy Spirit. Even to accomplish the material work ordered by God, the Spirit is more useful than material means. Of course Solomon would also need plenty of money, but not in first place. The Lord continues: "Because you . . . have not asked for yourself long life or riches or the life of your enemies, . . . behold, I now do according to your word. . . . I give you also what you have not asked, both riches and honor" (1 Kings 3:11-13).

"Seek first his kingdom and his righteousness," says Jesus, "and all these things shall be yours as well" (Mt 6:33). Provided, of course, we do not make God's kingdom an object of shrewd calculation, for God does not like schemers, and he never gives them what they have banked on.

Thus God asks Solomon the same question he asked Job and Abraham: Whom do you love? We know that after making this decision, Solomon becomes a powerful and wealthy king. He is not asked to give up his wealth; he does not have to make the same choice again. We cannot say that his righteousness as a wealthy man is exactly like that of Job and Abraham; in reality his wealth, like everything else in his and David's reigns, is a sign and a prophecy. He is not rich as an individual and for himself, but as king of the people of Israel and as prophet and representative of God.

His wealth is no more his own than was Job's. Nor do his justice and righteousness come from himself. Yet none of these come from the God of the past; rather they show forth the God who is coming. His wealth points to the kingdom of God which will be established with power and glory. His wealth allows Solomon to put together a strong army, to rebuild Jerusalem, to erect the Temple, to build a prodigious throne; and all this points only to that divine reality which humanity will see at the end of time. It points to the countless heavenly hosts of the Lord of hosts, the New Jerusalem, God's presence in all, his glorious throne, the throne of the Son of David returning to separate the living from the dead.

It was necessary to give humanity this pale reflection of God's power and glory and wealth. It was necessary for this son of David to show what the true Son of David, he who alone truly reflects God's glory, would be. This reflection was given to create hope. And Solomon's wealth was truly a living hope for Israel. Solomon exists only for this prophecy; it is the only thing that gives his life meaning. And consequently, if he is justified in his wealth, it is because this wealth is not his own but the kingdom of God's. He does not have the right to use it as he pleases; he cannot use it except as needed for the prophecy.

We nevertheless must note the bad effect this wealth had from a human point of view. The people of Israel are unhappier than ever. Abraham and Job as rich individuals could affirm that they had wronged nobody, that their wealth was not built on others' misery; but this cannot be the case when it is the king who becomes rich. The state bases its wealth on the work of its subjects, and the richer and more powerful it grows, the more its subjects are crushed by fees, taxes and forced labor. This is what happened in Solomon's case.

This should remind us that the curse of wealth is the same for the government as for an individual. We cannot expect to get rid of wealth's oppression by handing our riches over to the state. Solomon strongly disproves that. For if any government should have been able to avoid the bad effects of money, it was Solomon's because of its prophetic function. Scripture shows us, however, the other side of the picture. Humanity is not at all liberated by the wealth of the state, even if the state belongs to the son of David. And this reminds us of a general rule of prophecies: A prophetic act may be just, meaningful and important, but it is still a human act, which means it is sinful, incomplete and unjust. Prophecy is but a shadow of things to come, and the prophet's act represents only a part of what is to come; it does not show the whole picture. The wealthy Solomon is a prophet of the glory of the kingdom, but not at all of the joy and freedom of God's children. In fact, Solomon, by his very wealth, oppresses the children of Israel.

An Ethic of Wealth

We have just seen that the righteousness of wealth results not from a moral attitude but a spiritual one. Job and Solomon are not justified in being rich because they gained their wealth fairly or used it well. They are justified because of their relationship with God, a relationship of obedience, love and prophecy. Beyond that, the fact that they are rich brings good or bad consequences that have nothing to do with *their* righteousness or *their* morality. Nevertheless there is in the Old Testament an entire ethic of wealth which we cannot completely ignore.

Wealth Belongs to God. The starting point of this ethic is the fact that wealth belongs to God, whether or not this is obvious. It would seem that this observation would bring all discussion to a close. But nothing in human life or in spiritual reality is all that cut-and-dried.

God, however, as the true owner of wealth, disposes of it as he pleases. He gives it to whom he chooses, and it is his wisdom that decides—the wisdom concerning which Solomon said, "Long life is in her right hand; in her left hand are riches and honor" (Prov 3:16). We absolutely cannot argue with God about this. He is free, and he enriches or impoverishes as he pleases. Hannah, in her prayer for the gift of Samuel's birth, recalls this forcefully: "The LORD makes poor and makes rich; he brings low, he also exalts. He raises up the poor from the dust; he lifts the needy from the ash heap, to make them sit with princes" (1 Sam 2:7-8).

All we can do is accept God's decision; indeed, all the devout must do is recognize God's sovereignty. This recognition is the beginning of a right attitude toward wealth. David says in his last prayer: "O LORD our God, all this abundance that we have provided for building thee a house for thy holy name comes from thy hand and is all thy own" (1 Chron 29:16). His words are striking. He collected silver, precious woods, all the wealth necessary to build this temple; he took all necessary human measures; and having done this, he declared that God had given all this. Thus, even when wealth seems to be entirely the fruit of human labor, God asks for the same recognition of his sovereignty.

This is the vital point made by the writer of Ecclesiastes and by the prophets. Says the Preacher: "Every man also to whom God has given wealth and possessions and power to enjoy them, and to accept his lot and find enjoyment in his toil—this is the gift of God" (Eccles 5:19). The prophets constantly remind us that judgment falls on the person who does not recognize this reality. Ezekiel speaks against the Prince of Tyre because he credits his wealth to himself. Hosea says, "She did not know that it was I who gave her the grain, the wine, and the oil, and who lavished upon her silver and gold which they used for Baal" (Hos 2:8).

Here we confront a dilemma from which we cannot escape. Either we recognize that gold and silver belong to God, or we refuse to recognize this. But a refusal is not at all the objective, realistic attitude we too easily think it to be. Once we have rejected God's lordship over riches, we are no longer neutral about economic or moral questions. We cannot simply strip away the mythological layer to leave the naked scientific truth. We are not left alone to choose between good and evil in our use of wealth. For in reality, to reject God's lordship is, without any other possibility or third option, to submit this wealth to the Baal of this world, to the power of Satan. And if in the New Testament riches are part of Satan's kingdom, it is because the chosen people stopped recognizing God's glory in the form of wealth and started thinking of wealth as valuable in itself. Thus they gave it to Satan to dispose of from then on. But Jesus Christ, who alone knows the truth, refuses to accept wealth from this supposed new master.

The concept that wealth belongs to a higher power is not only the starting point of the Old Testament wealth ethic, it is also its boundary because no moral precepts make sense apart from this idea of ownership. We could practice all sorts of moral precepts without justifying wealth, for morality is an expression of justice only when it gives outward form to our recognition that wealth belongs to God. If we do not recognize that wealth belongs to God, outwardly moral behavior is only an expression of our *hypocrisy*.

It is not for nothing that hypocrisy is often linked with wealth in the Bible. As a matter of fact, the rich man of virtue gives us one of our clearest examples of hypocrisy. The rich man who behaves well thinks he is righteous, yet not his conduct but the very fact that he is rich makes him, in biblical thought, unrighteous. His unrighteousness ceases only when he puts all his wealth in God's hands, when he becomes poor (in the sense that we will develop in chapter five), an act which results from his recognition of God's ownership of his wealth.

As long as a person scrupulously observes God's commands concerning wealth, without however going to the heart of the problem, the law plays the role perfectly described by Paul. It is an instrument of death, a power of sin, for it spotlights our hypocrisy—the divorce between our outer actions, which make us believe we are righteous, and our inner revolt, which makes us refuse God's righteousness.

This is true for all people who possess money.

All people? Let us not forget that all this is spoken to Israel, for whom wealth has a particular meaning, as we shall see.

Even though it is only the first step, the first specifically moral commandment reveals some skepticism about human activity with regard to wealth, and tends to moderate the desire for riches. On the one hand, it is not worth submitting oneself to backbreaking labor in order to produce wealth; on the other hand, even if one recognizes its source, there is no point in asking God for it. God does not listen to the prayer whose purpose is gaining wealth. Doubtless it is God who gives it, but as Jesus proclaims, "Seek first his kingdom and his righteousness, and all these things shall be yours as well."

Such is already the situation under the old covenant. Scripture reports Solomon's prayer twice, and God answers him: "Because you have not asked for riches but for wisdom, ... I will give you riches *also*." In God's sight, it is not right to desire money. The only possible prayer about money is given to us in the well-known text of Proverbs (30:8): "Give me neither poverty nor riches." But not only are we not to beg God for wealth or even for the financial prosperity of our enterprises; numerous texts show us that it is not even worthwhile to dedicate our work toward producing riches.

Objections that these restraints on wealth are based on cultural differences are invalid, as are those that suggest that the Israelites—first nomads, then farmers—did not know or value money as wealth and that their judgment was conditioned by their social situation. Most of these Old Testament texts, in fact, come rather late, dating from a time when Israel is well established, in contact with rich neighbors (Tyre), trading with representatives of hellenistic civilization. Besides, Israel had already experienced wealth during Solomon's reign. Judgment is passed then for quite the opposite reason: because Israel's situation allowed the accumulation of wealth, because the problem existed and because many were likely feeling the attraction of riches.

Moreover, this is not a social or economic judgment, but one based on spiritual or ethical motives and on a particular understanding of human nature. Wealth is vanity: "Do not toil to acquire wealth; be wise enough to desist. When your eyes light upon it, it is gone; for suddenly it takes to itself wings, flying like an eagle toward heaven" (Prov 23:4-5). And we also know that the desire for wealth leads frequently, if not necessarily, to dishonesty: "He that maketh haste to be rich shall not be innocent" (Prov 28:20 KJV).

This then shows that the problem is not only with the means but also with the end of human activity and labor, for this work can never be consecrated to the annihilation of wealth. Note too that no distinction is made between collective and personal riches. The Jews had known times of collective ownership; if the wilderness ideal was a live issue with them, as the prophets seem to testify, if the vaunted poverty refers to the wilderness life, why not distinguish between privately owned wealth and wealth held by the people or the nation? Yet Solomon's riches, although admired and recognized as willed by God, were nevertheless surrounded with disapproval. In Scripture, the dangers of possessing great wealth are the same for the group as for the individual.

The Temptation of Wealth. Wealth is, in any event, a temptation—not an evil in itself, but a temptation. And we must never forget what temptation is in the context of the Fall. Only one temptation, Adam's, has ever been unadulterated. Since that time, the Fall has given temptation extraordinary power. Human beings, because of their nature, are not upright when faced with temptation; they usually succumb to it because they are evil and have no strength in themselves to resist. Because we are under the law of the Fall, we now fall every time, as if there were a spiritual law of gravity. Thus, to say that wealth is a temptation is to say that it is not neutral. It exists in relation with man, and this relation does not show our great spirituality or value. Rather, it shows our propensity to evil. Wealth is an occasion for downfall. We have two indications of this.

First, wealth is temptation because it urges us to put our confidence in money rather than in God. This is a well-known theme which is repeated in the New Testament. We do not need to press the point, for it is a self-evident truth: a person who has a strong point, whatever it may be, tends to ascribe his love, his hope and his security to it. For human beings prefer what they can see and touch to what God promises and gives (compare Ps 49:6-7; 52:7; 62:10). And it appears that we cannot do otherwise. Possessing wealth, money or worldly goods of whatever sort, we settle back and say, "My soul, enjoy yourself, for you have many possessions." It is almost impossible to have many possessions and remain righteous. Righteousness is total dependence on God's action.

What is more, material abundance leads man to defy God. Not only to neglect him, but to deny him. This is the second aspect of temptation: "Give me [not] riches; . . . lest I . . . deny thee, and say, 'Who is the LORD?' " (Prov 30:8-9). When we are satisfied, our hearts swell with pride (Hos 13:6). We need only remember God's long complaint against the Prince of Tyre reported by Ezekiel. God gives riches in creation and we seize them and make them our own; instead of giving glory to God, we glorify ourselves. Sheltered by our riches, we quickly mistake ourselves for God.

This is exactly what we see in today's exploding economic development. There is so much wealth in the world that even the poor share the mindset of the rich. Each of us says in the bottom of his heart: "Who is comparable to *man*? He has dominated the forces of nature, he has accumulated riches and has produced everything imaginable. *Man* is rich. And even if I am not rich myself, I ought to be, for I am human, and who is comparable to *me*?"

This great temptation permits us to mock God today as in the time of the prophets. What do we still need from God? Not only are we powerful, but we also claim to be righteous and just. "Ephraim said: 'Surely I have become rich, I have found wealth for myself; in all my labors they will find in me no iniquity, which would be sin' " (Hos 12:8 NASB). The good, respectable, hard-working person—this is our civilization's argument. All these riches surrounding us are simply the fruit of human labors. The only debate between capitalists and communists is over the ownership of these riches. But nobody asks if wealth itself is right and good, for in everyone's eyes, the person who has worked for them is upright.

Unfortunately, this is not God's judgment. To the person who declares, "I have found wealth for myself," God answers, "I am the LORD your God" (Hos 12:9). This response does not ignore the question; rather it answers it exactly. When we try to affirm our independence, God affirms his own sovereignty. We want to justify our wealth by our work. Now a person is justified, as we well know, by something greater than he is. The accused person does not justify himself; the judge justifies him. Thus a person declares himself just by appealing to something which justifies him, to a superior power. In this case it is his work. We are now in a position to understand the command which constantly recurs in God's Word: "You shall not worship the work of your hands." Among other things, this means "Do not try to justify yourself by your work." Thus whenever a person who has acquired great wealth claims to be just and righteous because his riches are the fruit of his labor, he is not appealing to natural law or operating in moral categories. He is instead defying God; he has entered the spiritual realm; he is committing the sin of rejecting God's lordship.

It is a difficult position to be in, for we have no way to get out of it. Either we gain our wealth by unjust means and find ourselves condemned by that fact, or we claim to be just and are equally condemned by the very justice of our means. Real life offers no other alternative. To be sure, philosophers can imagine hypothetical situations that are different, for this dilemma is neither a logical nor a biblical necessity. But if we wish to go by the truth of the real world and not by our imaginations or more or less invented possibilities, we say, "Things could be otherwise, but in fact they are like this." We are *truly* (not hypothetically) in this dilemma as a result of our nature. And in Scripture God tells us, not that it *must* be like this, but that it actually *is* like this, because this is how God sees our human situation.

Acquiring and Using Wealth. This does not mean, however, that the specifically moral aspect of wealth is ignored. The Bible does indeed provide criteria and instruction concerning good and bad ways to acquire and use wealth, and we must reckon with these also. But we must always remember that these criteria will not allow us to distinguish between the righteous rich man and the unrighteous one. When we read in Proverbs, "Wealth obtained by fraud dwindles, but the one who gathers by labor increases it" (Prov 13:11 NASB), we observe that this is common wisdom about a natural phenomenon, and not justice or righteousness in God's eyes nor the sure destiny of humankind.

It is not because riches are ill gained that they provoke condemnation, and it is not their fair acquisition that will lead to justification.

"Good" and "bad" methods of acquiring wealth are confirmed on earth at the human level: the person whose deeds are evil will sooner or later reap the consequences on earth, although evil is not always repaid by equal evil, and natural consequences do not inevitably follow. But no profound truth is involved here. As many other texts show, even if the wicked get rich and prosper, that says nothing at all about justice or about God's existence or power. Popular proverbs can handle this ordinary experience, if it is taken as a whole: "Like the partridge that gathers a brood which she did not hatch, so is he who gets riches but not by right; in the midst of his days they will leave him, and at his end he will be a fool" (Jer 17:11). This conviction is found frequently in the Old Testament; ultimately the wicked are punished, perhaps on earth, but most probably by death. "You can't take it with you." We constantly hear this wise warning; it is an important conviction, but it is not the most crucial lesson.

In addition, the problem of the proper use of wealth is raised, once again on legalistic and moralistic grounds. The wealthy have duties toward others and God. Job lists them: to care for the poor, to consider the needs of people, animals and even things. The rich have a potential that allows them to understand and assist the unfortunate. This is the true price of wealth. This is the only good use they can make of it. Scripture goes even further and speaks of the rights of the poor over the rich. Consider the powerful text in Proverbs where King Lemuel reminds us that the prince must maintain the rights of the afflicted, the "sons of misery," and that he must give them their rights[2] (Prov 31:5 French). Thus when the rich give, they acquire no virtue, no merit; they are only doing their duty. For to give to the poor is only to grant them their rights. Because they are "sons of misery," the poor have rights over the rich, and whenever they are denied their rights, God's justice must intervene to reestablish them. This is one of the foundations of the curse

---

[2]I have already stressed this characteristic of the claims of the poor, which is one of the foundations of law, in *The Theological Foundation of the Law*.

on the wealthy.

Finally this text tells us that the rich person's action on behalf of the poor cannot be a chance, fleeting, unusual occurrence. Rather the prince must *"maintain* the rights of the poor." Thus a fundamental relationship is established, and it is our duty not to avoid it.

And of course we cannot forget the great law of serving God. "Honor the LORD with your substance and with the first fruits of all your produce" (Prov 3:9). Our first duty is to recognize that God is the master of wealth. The idea is common enough. Christians must know that we are no more than humble stewards and that God is the true proprietor. Christians never own their possessions in the juridical and Roman sense of the term. At best they are only stewards who work on others' lands and who will have to give account to a master. I have already shown the tight limits within which this theory of stewardship must be kept, that it is not the key to all difficulties and that it presents plenty of dangers. It does not permit us to settle the problem of wealth. Does our position as stewards authorize us to develop, without measure, the goods entrusted to us? For whether stewards or not, our appetite for power constantly pushes us to make our money increase. Is a just use of money also a limited one?

In any case, just use does not permit anyone to take authority over others or over the Word of God. The prophets denounced these two serious ways of abusing wealth. God condemns Israel "because they sell the righteous for silver, and the needy for a pair of shoes" (Amos 2:6). The rich do not have the right to take possession of the poor. They do not have the right to lay hands on them or to reduce them to servitude because of money. As soon as money, one way or another, allows one person to dominate another, it is condemned. This takes aim at capitalism which, in both boss-worker and seller-buyer relations, establishes a relationship of domination based on money.

Condemnation also weighs heavily on the rich who either obtain social privilege or try to use God's Word to their own ends. For judges and priests are as susceptible as others to the temptation of money. "Its heads give judgment for a bribe, its priests teach for hire, its prophets divine for money; yet they lean upon the LORD" (Mic 3:11). The danger here is obviously not what we usually call injustice; it is not even the corruption of priests. It is enlisting God's Word in the service of money. Here we had better take a good look at our churches and ask if the Word of God is free with respect to capitalists who support the church. Is it free with respect to church organization which is built on money?

Obviously this also depends on recognizing God's sovereignty over possessions. But we observe that the Old Testament texts, when speaking of the good or bad use of wealth, allude to strictly earthly sanctions. It is the same when they speak of acquiring wealth by just or unjust means.

Again the moral problem is solved without reference to salvation and eternal life: when we do not recognize the source and true owner of our wealth, God takes it back (Hos 2:8-9). Inversely, if we recognize him, then "the threshing floors shall be full of grain, the vats shall overflow with wine and oil" (Joel 2:24). This is certainly not a primitive, materialistic conception of divine recompense. We must not forget that the prophets, who according to historians "spiritualized" Israel's religion, formulated these sanctions. Nevertheless it is not simply a metaphor either and cannot be purely and simply interpreted in a "higher" sense. It most definitely has to do with the normal result of a wise use of wealth.

But to have the correct view of this wise use, we must continually place our behavior in the perspective of the value and the nonvalue of wealth. Here again we find opposing texts, some affirming that wealth is useful and indispensable; others that it is vanity. We must situate all that is said about the acquisition and use of possessions in the exchange —one could almost say the dialog—between these viewpoints.

It is not surprising that we find most of the favorable statements about wealth in the book of Proverbs. "A rich man's wealth is his strong city" (Prov 10:15). And we surely must not deny the facts. The rich person is mistaken to think he is safe, but in everyday life, which we must see as it is, it is true that wealth is a protection; it is true that "money is the answer to everything," as the author of Ecclesiastes says (10:19 NASB). What is wrong with that? It is a normal consequence that we have no need to reject.

It is the same with the statement that riches procure many friends. This also is a fact. And it is very pleasant to have friends, security and comfort. But once we have observed this, we still have the warning (not the moral judgment but the warning) that all this is very fragile. The statement, "A rich man's wealth is his strong city," which is presented in Proverbs 10 without reticence as an all-embracing truth, is repeated in chapter 18 with this addition: "*in his imagination* it is like a high wall" (Prov 18:11, margin). And how often the maxims in Proverbs remind us that the rich person's friends disappear as soon as his money is gone.

There is no reason to complain about the economic crisis or human ingratitude. This is normal, these texts tell us. Just as it is normal to find security and happiness in wealth (and what harm is there in that?), it is also normal for one's fortune to collapse—this is part of its nature—and *it is normal for everything based on wealth to disappear with it*. The only mistake is to count on wealth, to be convinced that what one builds with gold and silver is solid, to believe that a virtuous use of possessions protects them.

Ultimately riches are useless; when all is said and done, this is the dominant affirmation: "He who loves money will not be satisfied with money" (Eccles 5:10).

Money and Desire. It is, moreover, instructive to note that the Hebrew word for money, *kesef,* comes from a verb meaning "to desire, to languish after something." This implies, first, that from the beginning, when the Hebrew language was being formed, the spiritual character of money as well as its power was already stressed. Later economic or theological developments did not bring us to this; right from the beginning this has been the (revealed) understanding of money. If money had been only an unimportant, secondary instrument in the primitive Hebrew economy, it would not have been given this name. Even though from an economic standpoint money was secondary in that era, its human force and spiritual reality were already recognized.

Second, this relation between money and desire shows that lust for money dwells within us. However much money we acquire, we are never satisfied; we always long for more. We must not understand this in the trite sense that no one ever has enough money, that the person who has wealth always wants more. Ecclesiastes 5:10 goes much further indeed: a person's hunger for money is always the sign, the semblance of another hunger—for power or rank or certainty. The love of money is always the sign of another need—to protect oneself, to be a superman, for survival or for eternity. And what better means to attain all this than wealth? In our frantic, breathless search, we are not looking for enjoyment alone. We are looking, without realizing it, for eternity. Now money does not satisfy our hunger nor respond to our love. We are on the wrong road. We have used the wrong means.

This is the first vanity of wealth, and the second is close to it: "Riches do not profit in the day of wrath" (Prov 11:4). "Men . . . trust in their wealth, . . . [but] truly no man can ransom himself, or give to God the price of his life" (Ps 49:6-7). There is one thing that wealth does not permit us to buy: ourselves. The slave cannot pay the price of freedom. There is no ransom from God's wrath or from demons. And wealth is vain if it does not ultimately do the one favor that matters, if it does not permit the one transaction that could tempt us! This psalm concludes that the rich who stake their whole lives on their wealth are "like the beasts that perish." This is not an abstract speculation or a vision of wealth from afar. Rather it concerns an extremely present and pressing reality; this is no spiritualization of wealth. Each person faces death; each person faces judgment; everyone is forced to weigh his wealth and has no choice but to judge its value. All our make-believe does not change reality. Thus, ultimately, wealth is vanity.

We are tempted to think that all this is simple and well known. It is true that we are looking at moral wisdom that is rather obvious, that makes sense. We do not expect much of it because it has never led anywhere. We are also tempted to think that this prayer to be preserved both from riches and from misery is exactly the "golden mean" which certain ancient philosophers made the criterion of virtue.

But in fact these biblical truths must absolutely not be isolated on the one hand from the other texts that put wealth in quite a different light, for biblical revelation forms a whole, and on the other hand from the person who gives this revelation, namely, God. These texts do not express human wisdom but God's action, not only God's will but also an action that is steadfastly pursued. Each of these apparently moralistic texts is inserted into the framework of God's action: God is taking possession of us and our works by placing us and our riches in precisely the dilemma (all or nothing) that we are trying to use our wealth to avoid. But we find ourselves constantly being led back to it.

Wealth as Reward and Blessing

Here we come to the heart of the problem. We know that one of the distortions of the Reformation was to assume that since work is a calling, the wealth that sanctions faithful work must confirm that calling. Even further, wealth is God's action in our life, showing divine approval and blessing. Those whom God blesses make a fortune. And soon the corollary was established: those who make a fortune are blessed by God. This can be quite orthodox if it is taken to mean that the person who makes a fortune does so by God's grace, but more often it is thought to mean that the person who makes a fortune thereby earns justification and sanctification. This is no exaggeration. It is a distortion of Calvinism, but this opinion can be supported by a great number of biblical texts; it might even be considered a faithful expression of Old Testament teachings.

And it is also, to some extent, although more discreetly, the opinion of the Israelites. If social success is a characteristic of Israel, if gentile wealth passes into the hands of the chosen people, this is neither an accident nor an undesirable characteristic of the race; it is the exact fulfillment of God's promises in the Old Testament. It is pointless to use historical circumstances to explain that which is better explained by a concern to fulfill God's promise (even if today this concern has been forgotten by most). For indisputably God's allocation of wealth is presented in the Old Testament as a reward and a blessing.

Wealth as Reward. It is seen as a reward, for example, in the Chronicles, a careful record of God's justice on earth. Jehoshaphat walked in the ways of David his father; he was devout and just. He did not seek the Baals, but destroyed them; he "sought the God of his father and walked in his commandments." Therefore God approved his faithfulness by giving him wealth: "The LORD established the kingdom in his hand . . . and he had great riches and honor" (2 Chron 17:4-5). And as a result of this wealth, moreover, we see that this king became even more devout and used his riches justly.

The same thing happened with Hezekiah, king of Judah, also a devout king. He revived the institution of Passover, among other things. And it is not without reason that we are told of Hezekiah's riches after the great crisis of his reign. After the miraculous deliverance of the kingdom, Hezekiah fell sick. God comforted him by giving him a sign, but Hezekiah did not show his gratitude. He "did not make return according to the benefit done to him." Then God was angered against him: "Therefore wrath came upon him and Judah and Jerusalem." Hezekiah, in the midst of his pride, humbled himself, and in response to the king's humiliation, God gave him considerable riches (2 Chron 32).

We have already emphasized the problem of purely earthly reward, but here something else is in question. The Proverbs speak of the natural consequences of a good use of wealth: if you use your possessions justly, they will increase. But in the examples we have just given, and in many other cases, wealth is a reward for piety, for faithfulness to God, for obeying his will; in other words, for a spiritual attitude. Wealth, then, appears to be a reward for spiritual righteousness. We are no longer talking about an accurate balance scale weighing out equity in material things; we are talking about God's eternal decrees.

This is even clearer when we consider all the promises to give wealth to Israel and, which often seems shocking, to hand over the wealth of other nations to Israel. Proverbs speaks in general terms about this: "The sinner's wealth is laid up for the righteous" (Prov 13:22). It is proof of God's justice which restores that which should be, but we must not forget that the just or righteous person in the Old Testament (as in the New) is the one who is justified by God: most of all, the people of Israel.

This comes to pass when, as they leave Egypt, the Jewish people seize considerable riches abandoned by the terrified Egyptians. The watchword "You will spoil the Egyptians" is fulfilled, and the same transfer of wealth takes place when the Israelites arrive in the land of Canaan. "I gave you a land on which you had not labored, and cities which you had not built, and you dwell therein; you eat the fruit of vineyards and oliveyards which you did not plant" (Josh 24:13).

This is the description of what Israel will continue to find if it is faithful. And while this shows the graciousness of God's gift to the righteous, it is also a brutal fact that God strips the unfaithful of the fruit of their labors in order to give it to the just. The riches amassed by the world seem by rights to belong to the person designated by God, and this shocks our sense of fairness and distributive justice.

This idea is repeated throughout Scripture, in the law (Deuteronomy), in the prophets (Amos and Micah) and in the writings (Proverbs and Job). And it seems to hold true for all time periods. It is therefore neither a one-time occurrence nor an incomplete stage in Israel's thought. When Job, in his last response, forcefully describes this situation, he reveals a permanent truth about Israel: "This is the portion of a wicked man with God. . . . Though he heap up silver like dust, and pile up clothing like clay; he may pile it up, but the just will wear it, and the innocent will divide the silver" (Job 27:13, 16-17). We are thus led to consider this arbitrary act of God not only as a reward for the righteous, but also as a blessing—in other words, an allocation of grace which, as we well know, God gives with no motive other than his love. We will see later how we should understand this.

Wealth as Blessing. A whole collection of biblical passages attests that the allocation of wealth is a blessing in the full sense of the term. It is even a part of the blessing on Abraham and his descendants. After the meeting between Abraham and Melchizedek, the promise of Canaan is made. First of all Abraham has a vision; then after preparing the sacrifice, he has a dream. And it is by means of this dream that God reveals to him the destiny of the chosen people. In the midst of this promise we read: "They will be oppressed, . . . but . . . afterward they shall come out with great possessions" (Gen 15:13-14). It is thus part of the fundamental blessing on Israel. We can be certain that this is not an unimportant bit of information, and if throughout Israel's history we find specific indications of the wealth which should belong to them, this is not accidental. It is a reference to this original blessing, a reminder of their election and a tangible sign that God's promise will one day be fulfilled.

Again we must note that the wealth mentioned here has an ambiguous nature. Nothing indicates that material riches are being spoken of; this is not necessarily money, even though the word used is the usual one. It could be that this amazing promised wealth is the revelation at Sinai. The way it is mentioned makes us realize that its nature is, at least, ambiguous. This promise was undoubtedly not fulfilled in the material sense as soon as the Israelites left Egypt.

But we meet it again in the blessings and curses right at the end of the wilderness wandering, just as they are about to enter the Promised Land and possess the first object of the promise. This is said as a blessing: "The LORD your God will make you abundantly prosperous in all the work of your hand, in the fruit of your body, and in the fruit of your cattle, and in the fruit of your ground" (Deut 30:9). This much is unambiguous: the promised wealth is certainly material. It is a part of the exceptional system established by God to help his people.

The dying Moses refers to the promised wealth in his song, then in the prophetic benediction he pronounces over the tribes, especially Joseph and Naphtali. But in these texts we again find the ambiguity we saw in the revelation made to Abraham. And this allows us to say with assurance that the promised wealth goes beyond material riches, for wealth is above all a blessing from God. All these stories have to do with spiritual things, and we are sure that the promise, which certainly has a material component, goes beyond merely material things.

The promise to Israel is expanded and apparently turned into a general principle valid for everyone in the later writings, especially in the major prophets and the Proverbs. But the ambiguity we have already pointed out is maintained. We find a representative phrase in Proverbs: "The blessing of the LORD makes rich" (Prov 10:22). We do not know if in this text the blessing of the Lord means material riches, with wealth being the expression of this blessing, or if the blessing is itself the object of value. In the latter case, we could despise material possessions as false wealth. True wealth would be found in the blessing alone, and it should be protected as the most precious of our possessions. It is not carelessness to say that both interpretations are possible: indeed I believe that, rather than contradicting each other, they overlap and are complementary.

But two parallel texts we can cite are much more obviously concerned with eternal reward and the total blessing on the wise and good: "The crown of the wise is their riches" (Prov 14:24 NASB—and of course we must remember that *crown* has a spiritual meaning; it represents sharing in the glory of God; it is the manifestation of God in someone's life), and "The reward for humility and fear of the LORD is riches and honor and life" (Prov 22:4). The terms are exactly parallel. The fear of the Lord is the beginning of wisdom; he who fears can already be called wise.

God's response to this fear and this wisdom is wealth (a form of sharing in his glory) or wealth and honor.

And here again we are struck, in the list in the second text, with this mixture of sacred and profane things, of spiritual and material gifts: riches, honor, life. For these three terms can and, I believe, must be taken in two ways. On the one hand they have the material meaning of an abundance of money, political honor (as in Solomon's case) and concrete life; on the other, the spiritual meaning of an abundance of grace, sharing in God's glory and eternal life. We must never spiritualize revelation, but neither must we deny its spiritual sense. The unity of the two senses forces us not to limit this benediction to wealth, or more accurately, not to consider wealth itself as the blessing. The two are in close relationship, but by itself, the abundance of possessions is nothing.

God does not necessarily attach his blessing to this sign. We know Job's struggle in which he had to learn that God's blessing was upon him in spite of his misery; wealth and blessing are not strictly equivalent. We must nevertheless point out that, once Job understood this, God gave him even greater wealth.

In reality, God uses this exterior sign to call us to recognize that he is truly the Lord of heaven and earth; he calls us to recognize him as the God who gives and who gives himself abundantly.

This is the import of this relationship between wealth and blessing. Wealth is never considered in and of itself; it is never a value. And it is precisely because wealth is joined to blessing, because it is the sign of this reality, that there is shock and protest in the pages of the Old Testament whenever wealth is given to a bad or unjust person.

Wealth as Scandal. Now of course wealth as such can be given to a bad person. The psalmist and Job let their indignation ring out. In their eyes it is almost a sacrilege, because the sign receives (wrongly) the dignity of the thing for which it stands. "Behold, these are the wicked; always at ease, they increase in riches. All in vain have I kept my heart clean" (Ps 73:12-13). "Put no confidence in extortion, set no vain hopes

on robbery; if riches increase, set not your heart on them" (Ps 62:10).
"Why do the wicked live, reach old age, and grow mighty in power? . . .
No rod of God is upon them. . . . They spend their days in prosperity.
. . . They say to God, 'Depart from us! We do not desire the knowledge
of thy ways. What is the Almighty, that we should serve him? And what
profit do we get if we pray to him?' " (Job 21:7-15).

The scandal lies in the rich person's attitude toward God, the fact
that he affronts God and nevertheless remains rich, with the appearance of being blessed. This is not a case of economic jealousy, nor is it
religious materialism. It is a true scandal, a trap laid by Satan for us.
But it is a trap that God will ultimately use to teach us where God's sole
and entire blessing lies. When this happens, wealth receives another
destiny, another orientation.

A prophetic text pushes us further in the same direction. It concerns the great eschatological vision of Isaiah (60—61). Speaking to
Jerusalem, he announces its restoration as well as its complete communion with the Lord. "The glory of the LORD has risen upon you."
In this description, the destination of wealth is revealed to us: "you
shall see and be radiant, your hearts shall thrill and rejoice; because
the abundance of the sea shall be turned to you, the wealth of the nations
shall come to you. . . . All those from Sheba shall come. They shall bring
gold and frankincense, and shall proclaim the praise of the LORD. . . .
For the coastlands shall wait for me, the ships of Tarshish first, to bring
your sons from far, their silver and gold with them, for the name of the
LORD your God" (Is 60:5-6, 9). At the same time, this prophecy sheds
light on the shocking promise that Israel will be given wealth acquired
by others.

Is this text of Isaiah, so characteristically spiritual, a spiritualization
of the ancient Jewish attitude, or is it only a development of it? In other
words, did the ancient Hebrews consider wealth itself a blessing? Isaiah,
unable to accept this doctrine, helps Jewish thought evolve in the direction of "sign." From this time forward, wealth is not more than a tan-

gible gift representing a future spiritual gift of far greater import. Is this idea, which coincides with other texts (such as Ps 49:17), the fruit of more developed thought, of a higher conception of justice and right-eousness on the part of Israel? This interpretation is common among historians, but could not one think just as legitimately that the ambiguity observed above is evidence that, from the beginnings of Jewish thought, an openness to this interpretation has been possible? In that case Isaiah would have modified nothing of the original revelation, but would only have expressed it more clearly and developed it further.

Before answering this question, we must look at another story: the story of Jacob's prosperity. The cheater seizes great wealth by extremely dubious methods, but because he lives by grace as part of God's plan, he keeps these riches (Gen 31). They are undoubtedly illegitimate; they have been gained by fraud, and the way he uses them is not very praise-worthy, but these riches are nevertheless the sign of what already belongs to him. He is the bearer of grace and of the promise. His wealth is worth nothing by itself. Jacob is not seen from the standpoint of morality.

The ethical principles of which we have spoken have nothing to do with Jacob's adventures. These principles are expressed by Laban's sons, who think (rightly, humanly speaking) that they have been cheated; but if they punished Jacob as he deserved for his theft, they would be going against God's will. In reality, when Jacob acted as he did, he was seizing the sign of the promise; he was grabbing the guarantee that the promise was made to him. And if the means he used are totally unsanctified (Jacob is still a sinner, and the condemnation of the rich reappears here), nevertheless the meaning he gives to his success is according to God's will.

Wealth as a Sacrament

Unless we look at wealth only from the moral point of view, and we have already seen the limitations of this viewpoint, it is impossible to accept the materialistic interpretation which would give wealth intrinsic value in the Old Testament.

Background for seeing wealth as a sacrament is found in the account of the Promised Land. In the texts we have considered, it is inconceivable to apply the promise of Canaan to a politico-material matter. If we do not wish to twist them and touch them up arbitrarily, we have to recognize the duality in them. It is pointless to explain them by alluding to mythology or poetry or oriental exaggeration. In matters of revelation, the Jews used a careful vocabulary and precise forms which said exactly what they meant. These texts show God promising the Promised Land: from the beginning this implies two ideas (even if at first the Jews were not entirely aware of them).

First is the material event of giving a place to God's people. But neither God's purposes nor his mercy stops there; God vows that he will give, in the same manner, the kingdom. The Promised Land is not only the promise to enter Canaan, but also the promise to enter the kingdom. And to possess the Promised Land is to have in hand a proof that God's power, thus expressed, likewise assures us of our entrance into his kingdom. God's gift of this piece of earth is a down payment, a guarantee that he will establish the new creation, that he never stops working. But obviously there is no point in overvaluing the sign. We must cling to what the sign represents. And that is why we are constantly reminded to look to the past (where God awarded the Promised Land), *so that* we may more energetically march forward toward the kingdom. The characteristics of the Promised Land, moreover, are the very characteristics of the kingdom.

What is said about the relation between wealth and spirituality is comparable to what is said about the relation between the Promised Land and the kingdom. Wealth is never anything more than a sign of blessing, or more precisely, it is itself the blessing insofar as blessing is a sign of grace. To make a fortune never has any meaning unless the fortune is received as a sign of God's higher action. The person who sees this fortune as a blessing in itself and who thanks God for money (Zech 11:5) and the person who sees wealth as a uniquely material affair are equally in error. Wealth in the Old Testament is a proof and a down payment. It is proof that God who hands out material blessings, who gives them to whom he pleases, also gives grace. "Which is easier, to say, 'Your sins are forgiven you,' or to say, 'Rise and walk'?" (Lk 5:23). In the old covenant, the riches given by God are a proof of his spiritual action.

The person who receives riches receives in them proof that God *can* act in that manner, that God is in charge of the worldly powers, that he owns and commands them just like he owns and commands spiritual powers and, at a higher level, forgiveness and love. It is thus proof that God speaks the truth. The truth of God's promises is built on the fact that God *already* gives this wealth. We see then that wealth is a down payment; it is the first part of the fulfillment. God has promised grace, and he begins to fulfill this promise by acting in this material way. The person who accepts money as a sign holds a material object to which he can refer to assure himself that God's action for him has indeed begun. Thus the person realizes not only that God is able to do what he has promised, that he is Master of all that exists on earth and in heaven, but also that he *wants* to do this and that he has already begun his work.

This way of looking at wealth gives it the ability to symbolize grace. The person who receives riches knows that the Word spoken by God is also for him; this is how Abraham and Solomon understood it. We are tempted to say that this is a materialistic, stingy idea, that the person chosen by God has no need of these proofs and down payments. We must always be careful not to spiritualize man and God's action on his behalf. In reality, we know that we have great need of material signs, for we are only human even when we have been chosen by God. We have material bodies with all their inherent weaknesses and limitations. God chooses what best corresponds to the human body and appetite to use as an index of his true and profound action, which we can grasp only by analogy and reflection.

But we can still wonder why God chose wealth as a sacrament. For it seems evident, I think, that this is exactly how we ought to understand it, and if we wish to take another look at the texts we have cited in light of this definition, we will see that wealth corresponds to it exactly. Wealth is one of the sacraments of the old covenant. As a matter of fact, God's choice of this sign is not irrational. There is always some relationship between the sign and the thing signified, always a profound connection, as Jesus clearly shows with bread and wine. This relationship is here shown by the ambiguity of the texts.

The Things Signified. The gift of riches implies first that election is free, without charge. If we know, believe and are persuaded that our possessions, our money and fortune are nothing but things that have come from God, we cannot help being struck by the contrast between divine affirmation and human conviction. We are persuaded that we have earned our money, that it is the simple and direct fruit of our labors; whereas God declares that it is a free gift, that nothing would have come of the labor had God not given it. It is the same for election. We are convinced that our virtues and merits have made us worthy of being chosen by God; whereas God constantly repeats that there is no cause nor reason for this election, that it is a free decision of his love. Thus when we know that our wealth is a free gift, we become capable of grasping *also* that our eternal election is a free gift.

This is particularly significant for the Jewish people, the chosen people who constantly try to reappropriate this election and make it their own, as man tries to make money his personal property. Wealth should be for Israel a reminder that election is free. When wealth is taken away, this is also a sign that election depends on God alone. If God is faithful, it is because of his name and not because we own our possessions. And if the wealth continues, it is not in the natural order of things; it is a continuation of grace which, like wealth, is never our due nor guaranteed to us.

Second, the fact that wealth has been used as a sign implies that grace is given abundantly. God is not a miser who measures and counts out his grace. This is why the sign of grace is not a portion: a fragment of bread, a drop of wine, a piece of money. Abundant wealth is the sign, as in the feeding of the five thousand. When God gives grace he does not divide it up; he gives it in fullness. He covers all sins; he gives all his love; he opens the doors of eternity. And when he opens up the Promised Land, it is a land overflowing with wealth. He gives a measure that is heaped up and overflowing; grace does not stop with immediate needs, with the bare essentials. God does not restrict himself to daily bread; he gives wealth along with luxury, comfort, ease and of course the possibility of giving in return. And he gives us all this to teach us what is the grace that has been given us. This is another way in which wealth is different from money according to Scripture.

Third, this sacrament, like all sacraments, has a prophetic and eschatological meaning. We have already glimpsed this in Isaiah. The person who receives wealth already participates in the kingdom of God, into which all wealth will be gathered. We find, moreover, an amazing promise that all human accomplishment is not destined for destruction but will take its place in the heavenly Jerusalem (Is 60:3, 5; Rev 21:24-26). It will be a part of this Jerusalem. Not only will it somehow be brought up there; it belongs there according to God's will. Human wealth will embellish God's city; there it is enshrined and there it finds its place, its meaning, its truth and its irreplaceable character.

When we carefully read the Old Testament texts as well as those in Revelation, we realize that the holy city would miss our wealth if it were not taken there. The heavenly Jerusalem would not be complete if this wealth were absent. This implies that the enormous human effort to accumulate wealth is necessary for the re-creation that God will accomplish there. Of course, if this is the case, it is because God has chosen that it be so. We are not talking about natural necessity or about a necessity because God could not get along without human collaboration, because his power is limited or because his work is imperfect. No, God has willed that man participate, that mankind's works and wealth have their place. But because of this will, because of this free and independent decision of God who is subject to no necessity, if this wealth is missing, there will be a gap, an absence, a void in God's work.

Thus people ultimately build up wealth for God. And this, without any doubt, is what is meant by the idea that the wealth of the nations will be brought to Israel. To the extent that Israel focuses on Jerusalem, the image of the heavenly Jerusalem, we do not find a desire to conquer and to hoard in these texts or in Israel's history. This allocation to Israel takes place only when Israel is truly the Israel of God: "You shall be called the priests of the LORD, men shall speak of you as the ministers of our God; you shall eat the wealth of the nations, and in their riches you shall glory" (Is 61:6). This is certainly speaking of the time when God's people will really, totally and unhesitatingly be priests and servants. But not before. Now is this possible before the new creation exists? Isaiah seems to be making this transformation a sign of the New Jerusalem.

But wealth as an integral part of God's creation has one more characteristic of a sacrament: it makes the glory of the heavenly Jerusalem present in our midst. It is also a witness in our midst that this world, our work and the totality of human powers all belong to God. We must here argue from the other direction. Earlier we considered the idea that wealth was to be developed for its place in the New Jerusalem. Thus the person who accumulated riches was in a sense (even without knowing this) preparing material for God's work. But knowing this, we must begin with the heavenly Jerusalem and consider wealth in relation to it. What does it then mean, if not that wealth is already in our midst a basic element of God's work, that it is already its sign and its presence? Not that God will use *these* coins, *this* money, *these* precious stones in their concrete reality, but their concrete reality is the sign of what God will ultimately choose to use. Then wealth can in no way be seen as unimportant, since it is destined to remind us of such an important divine decision.

And this is indeed what we learn from Solomon's riches. Solomon, one of the rich men whose righteousness is recognized, is righteous only insofar as he is the prophet of Jesus Christ's glory. Prophet of glory—the idea assumes that all forms of human glory including wealth will ultimately be integrated in Christ's glory. It conversely assumes that Solomon's wealth, because it is prophetic, is in reality clothed with righteousness. But this is speaking of the wealth of Solomon, and certainly not that of Standard Oil.

Ethical Implications. If we accept the idea that wealth in the Old Testament is a sacrament (with the meanings we have just discussed), this leads to an ethic which is not strongly delineated in the texts but which is indicated only incidentally. Obviously the person who understands what wealth means, who like Abraham or Solomon receives it with thanksgiving and gratefulness, feels some sense of duty toward God in the way he handles this wealth.

If wealth is a sacrament standing for a spiritual reality, we must subordinate the thing to its meaning. We are therefore called to use our wealth so that our actions announce to the watching world that election is free, that grace is abundant, that a new creation is promised and that God owns all things. The important thing is never again the wealth itself or the social forces or economic power it represents, but only the spiritual reality to which it points. And we are disobedient when we attribute to wealth a value in itself, considering only how to use it and profit from it. We are disobedient when we give to the sign the full meaning of the reality, thus effacing and forgetting this reality.

This is easy to do when the sign itself has too much value. We sometimes speak of Hebrew materialism. Because both land and wealth have meaning, value, attractiveness and usefulness in themselves, it is easy enough to forget the spiritual meaning that lies behind the overly obvious and satisfying material meaning. Because wealth satisfies our understandable, enormous desires, it quickly loses its further, future meanings. We are satisfied when our body and heart are satisfied; we go to sleep then and do not search further. Wealth's ambivalence leads us, when material satisfaction becomes overly important, to attribute *all* importance to the sign and therefore to ourselves.

God keeps the situation ambiguous because Adam's situation after the Fall is ambiguous, but we try to destroy this ambiguity to our own profit by excluding the value God places on his action and his life. Likewise we get rid of the ambivalence of riches by eliminating the sacramental value God has given them, retaining only the economic and financial value. Hebrew materialism, then, is in no way the sign of a primitive mentality. It is the sign of human disobedience to a difficult order established by God, a refusal of the eschatological tension well typified in the ethical demand placed on us by God's evaluation of wealth.

But this tension can lead the opposite way when we accept God's direction. It can lead to a recognition that wealth is nothing because it has no meaning apart from God and that true wealth is God himself. Here again the ambivalence is suppressed, this time in God's direction, yet the suppression can never be complete because human nature presupposes attachment to wealth as such. Here the thing signified fills the whole picture and the sign no longer has any value. Thus we can abandon wealth as if it were unimportant, for where God is, gold means nothing and even loses its attractiveness as a human power. "If you lay gold in the dust, and gold of Ophir among the stones of the torrent bed, and if the Almighty is your gold, and your precious silver; then you will delight yourself in the Almighty, and lift up your face to God" (Job 22:24-26). This is ultimately where a true understanding of wealth must lead. But it does not appear that the people of the old covenant (any more than Christians) accepted this conclusion. God as our only wealth is not a sufficient guarantee, and people did not want to give to the thing signified what they too easily gave the sign. This is why a new era begins with Jesus Christ.

The Desacramentation of Wealth

Jesus Christ strips wealth of the sacramental character that we have recognized in the Old Testament. When Jesus is present, there is no room for this sacrament. This is an application of what we read in the letter to the Hebrews, that the old covenant was "a shadow of the good things to come" (Heb 10:1). But where the sun is, the shadow disappears. Jesus himself is abundant grace, free election, the presence of the kingdom. He is these things with a fullness that the people of Israel never knew. He is the faultless synthesis of all God's action.

It is therefore to be expected that everything intended to manifest this action to us and to remind us of it would be abolished. And as the sacrifices were set aside because of Jesus' sacrifice, so wealth no longer expresses spiritual truth because the fullness of grace resides in Christ. What would the gift of wealth mean now that God has given his Son? He is now our only wealth.

Within the line of God's action and succession of favors, where wealth looks like a personal favor and blessing given to one person in the midst of collective acts concerning the whole nation, a kind of regrouping and gathering take place. All the action culminates in the gift of the Son. All the favors, wealth included, are gathered up in this. There is no longer a difference between collective and personal grace. There is no longer any reason to signify one aspect of grace, for what is given to us in Jesus Christ henceforth has no common ground with all that wealth was able to express and to tell us.

Here is the principal reason for this rupture: henceforth wealth will be, with respect to Jesus Christ, a sign with no referent. Indeed wealth was a suitable sign in the Old Testament, because God's action toward his people was always manifested in specific material events. Whether the departure from Egypt or the conquest of the Promised Land, it always involved events with an immediate human and material character. From this we understand that wealth with all its human grandeur could play its assigned role: like a mirror, it could direct the light toward the point of God's action.

In Jesus Christ, however, God does not act by intervening in historical circumstances. Certainly his action is not only spiritual, and there is indeed historical intervention, but this is not an action with political or economic repercussions. Beginning with Jesus the sacrament must refer to a *specific* action of God: this then implies a sacrament that is more intimate, more personal and more directly tied to our lives; one that is less material, less visibly useful than wealth. Wealth, well suited to bringing the gift of the Promised Land to mind, is certainly not suited to reminding us of the gift of the Child in a manger. It is not an adequate sign; therefore we find it stripped of its true value.

God thus puts an end to the sign's ambiguity. Wealth is no longer a sacrament because "God chose what is weak in the world to shame the strong" (1 Cor 1:27). In Christ God chooses that which has no intrinsic value and makes it adequate to the work he is undertaking. This work must not be done by human hands. It must not be possible for anyone to thank a particular method for what is solely an action of grace. Wealth by itself is an economic power, and because it is a power, it is now rejected.

Not only can it no longer be the sign of the path of humility which God adopts in Jesus Christ, it is directly opposed to that path. As soon as wealth stops being a sign, everything is changed, for it then ceases to be historically integrated with God's work. We give it a value, and it is only for this value that it will be considered from now on. All meaning that it took from its relationship with God, who made it a blessing, disappears. It is no longer a sign, no longer a blessing, now that Jesus Christ is our reality as well as our blessing. It is thus returned to its natural grandeur. And that is why the New Testament authors speak of money with severe realism. Other sacraments have replaced the old ones, other blessings will bring us more than we ever could have hoped. The former things have passed away.

Wealth, then, is reduced to money. And money has no place in the work of redemption. Of course it has its role to play, but it is no longer the same, for money is not the same as wealth; one refers more to the idea of exchange, the other expresses more the idea of abundance. Their implications differ. In the New Testament, wealth is most often thought to be simply the accumulation of money. Therefore the rich hardly have a place in the work of redemption: "Consider your call, brethren; not many of you were . . . powerful, not many were of noble birth" (1 Cor 1:26). How could the rich join in stripping money of its power? Thus the Incarnation of Jesus Christ totally modifies our perspective. Nevertheless the eschatological thrust continues; all we have said about the place of wealth in the future Jerusalem is maintained and even developed. But money's historical destiny and man's ethical attitude toward money are changed to the extent that God stops giving wealth as a sign of spiritual truth. Yet all is not abolished. As a matter of fact, this also is a fulfillment. The implications of God's concrete provisions will be obvious once the material form of those provisions is stripped away and only the seed-bearing kernel, as Jesus Christ reveals it, remains.

CHAPTER THREE
MONEY

WHEN WE THINK ABOUT THE PROBLEMS MONEY CAUSES IN OUR society, we think in economic terms, and when we understand the problems it causes in our personal lives, we ask questions in moral terms.

This attitude, which is popular in our day, presupposes that money is an object. We easily identify money with currency or even monetary signs such as coins and bills. To have money is to have lots of cash, and by extension, it is to have investments or a bank account.

If this were our starting point, we would not need to write about money, for there are already many financial, economic or ethical studies on the subject and there would be no need for another one. But our point of view here is different. We are called to speak about money, not only because money plays a major role in our world, but also because the Bible speaks to us about it in a very specific way. If we accept this starting point, we must try to hear what the Bible says about it; we must speak of it *as* the Bible speaks.

What Money Really Is

Now, the Bible raises the moral problem only incidentally and gives ethical rules about money only secondarily. The Bible sees money differently from the way modern man sees it. In biblical texts money is only rarely spoken of as a neutral object without autonomy or self-generated action. Scripture seldom looks at money from a monetary standpoint.

Doubtless it raises the question of the ownership of money, but only to attest clearly that we are not the owner. We immediately assume that the owner is God. Only one text exists that has this meaning, Haggai 2:8, but it would be a mistake to invoke it. First, the phrase "The silver is mine, and the gold is mine" is speaking of precious metals and not necessarily of money as a means of exchange and capitalization. We must get rid of our too rapid identification of money with precious metals. It is a coincidence, not a necessity, that metals have been used to represent money. Other civilizations which have used money, sometimes in a very advanced way, have not known it in the form of gold. Thus the biblical texts speaking of gold and silver do not necessarily relate to our question. But in addition, a complete reading of Haggai shows that this is a prophecy with an eschatological fulfillment. It focuses on the moment when the heavens and the earth will be shaken, when all worldly treasures will come to the Temple and when peace will reign. Consequently, the meaning of this verse is not at all what we usually make it. We will have to come back to it later.

The other texts which speak of the ownership of money concern primarily the ownership of monetary symbols. In this category is Jesus' response to those who asked if it was necessary to pay taxes. Holding up a coin, he asks whose inscription it bears. The inscription indicates ownership, and Jesus, without discussion, grants ownership of the coin to Caesar, thus to the political power, the state (Mt 22:17-21). A nation's glory is found in whatever manifests the reality of its power, and this includes its monetary symbol. Thus when Satan leads Jesus up a mountain to tempt him, shows him the glory of all the kingdoms of the world and promises to give these kingdoms to him, he affirms that in the last analysis these monetary riches belong to him through Caesar.

But this problem of the ownership of money is still not at the heart of the question. Jesus raises the question in its fullness when he calls money *Mammon* (Mt 6:24; Lk 16:13), an Aramaic word that usually means "money" and also can mean "wealth." Here Jesus personifies money and considers it a sort of god. He does not get this idea from his cultural milieu. Jesus did not adopt a designation for money that was popular among his listeners, for it appears that neither the Jews and Galileans nor the nearby pagans knew a god by this name. Jesus did not use a pagan god to show that one must choose between the true God and a false god. No doubt though, as Martin Achard points out, the way this term is used in the Targums and in the Talmud is already somewhat personalized. For some of Jesus' contemporaries, Mammon is one of the elements of this world which are marked for destruction, to be annihilated in the Messianic era. But we hardly see in this usage of *Mammon* the idea of a power, and it is certainly not a personification. As far as we can tell from known texts, we can say that Jesus gives this term a force and a precision that it did not have in its milieu. This personification of money, this affirmation that we are talking about something that claims divinity (whether Jesus adopted it from the Ebionite milieu or whether he created it), reveals something exceptional about money, for Jesus did not usually use deifications and personifications.

What Jesus is revealing is that money is a power. This term should be understood not in its vague meaning, "force," but in the specific sense in which it is used in the New Testament. Power is something that acts by itself, is capable of moving other things, is autonomous (or claims to be), is a law unto itself, and presents itself as an active agent. This is its first characteristic. Its second is that power has a spiritual value. It is not only of the material world, although this is where it acts. It has spiritual meaning and direction. Power is never neutral. It is oriented; it also orients people. Finally, power is more or less personal. And just as death often appears in the Bible as a personal force, so here with money. Money is not a power because man uses it, because it is the means of wealth or because accumulating money makes things possible. It is a power *before* all that, and those exterior signs are only the manifestations of this power which has, or claims to have, a reality of its own.

We absolutely must not minimize the parallel Jesus draws between God and Mammon. He is not using a rhetorical figure but pointing out a reality. God as a person and Mammon as a person find themselves in conflict. Jesus describes the relation between us and one or the other the same way: it is the relationship between servant and master. Mammon can be a master the same way God is; that is, Mammon can be a personal master.

Jesus is not describing the particular situation of the miser, whose master is money because his soul is perverted. Jesus is not describing a relationship between us and an object, but between us and an active agent. He is not suggesting that we use money wisely or earn it honestly. He is speaking of a power which tries to be like God, which makes itself our master and which has specific goals.

Thus when we claim to use money, we make a gross error. We can, if we must, use money, but it is really money that uses us and makes us servants by bringing us under its law and subordinating us to its aims. We are not talking only about our inner life; we are observing our total situation. We are not free to direct the use of money one way or another, for we are in the hands of this controlling power. Money is only an outward manifestation of this power, a mode of being, a form to be used in relating to man—exactly as governments, kings and dictators are only forms and appearances of another power clearly described in the

Bible, political power. This comparison does not necessarily mean that money can be ranked with the "rule and authority and power and dominion" of which Paul speaks (Eph 1:21). But neither does anything require us to challenge this interpretation. Without proof to the contrary, it would seem reasonable to accept this identification.

That Mammon is a spiritual power is also shown by the way we attribute sacred characteristics to our money. The issue here is not that idols have been built to symbolize money, but simply that for modern man money is one of his "holy things." Money affairs are, as we well know, serious business for modern man. Everything else—love and justice, wisdom and life—is only words. Therefore we avoid speaking of money. We speak of business, but when, in someone's living room, a person brings up the topic of money, he is committing a social error, and the resulting embarrassment is really expressing the sense of the sacred. This is true for the middle class.

Among the working class we find the same sentiment, but in a different form: it is the widespread conviction that if the money question is solved, all problems of the working class and of humankind in general will thereby be solved as well. It is also the conviction that everything that does not tend to solve the money problem is only hot air. Although this holiness attributed to money can be expressed in many ways, it exists in the heart of everyone.

We understand then why money questions are not considered, in the Bible, as part of the moral order. They are actually part of the spiritual order. They have to do with relating to a power, and not with behavior toward an object. And the Old Testament texts about money must be read in this perspective. If we restrict them to their legal scope, they are nothing more than judicial rather than ethical provisions. But all of them refer to a higher reality. They all witness to another underlying problem, as we will see. And they can be understood only in the framework of the spiritual power of money.

What Money Does. This power of money establishes in the world a certain type of human relationship and a specific human behavior. It creates what could be broadly called a buying-selling relationship. Everything in this world is paid for one way or another. Likewise, everything can, one way or another, be bought. Such is the character that the power of money imposes on the world. Although money is only one means of this power's action, it is the most visible and concrete sign of the universality of buying and selling. The world sees this behavior as normal. Without constant exchange, we could not continue to live.

Now this takes on extremely diverse aspects; Scripture shows several of them. How can anything be exempt from the buying-selling relationship? Everything is bought, including human beings (Amos 2:6; 8:6). Once again, this is not a perversion or a situation peculiar to a particular civilization. It is the way the power of money works. Its most tangible form is what we call slavery, but we must realize that the poor person's situation is not much different from that of a slave. According to the Bible, it is extremely easy to slip from poverty into slavery. The purchase of a slave is the purchase not only of a body but of the whole person. Poverty also leads to the total alienation of the poor, an alienation which puts the labor force at the disposal of the wealthy, permitting the wealthy to impose their own law and conception of life, their own thought and religion.

Poverty leads to the total subjection of the poor, together with their family and inner life, to the rich. It is this purchase of the inner person, attested by the Bible, that corrupts the money relationship. The Bible stresses that the soul is bought (Rev 18:11-13). The real significance of this is that in such a sale, people are seen as objects. They are thus turned away from their true end, their purpose (to glorify God), and at the same time they are put under a false authority, one that is not God, whether this is directly or indirectly recognized.

A related example of the way money corrupts the inner person is betrayal for money. It is not insignificant that Judas's act is represented as a purchased act. It was necessary for the power of money to interfere and direct it. Betrayal is another example of our possession by this power. Judas's betrayal would not be complete if it were not the fruit of the conflict between Satan and Jesus, if it were not to all appearances a Satanic triumph. Satan had to bring all his powers into play: the power of violence with the soldiers, the power of the law with the high priest, the power of money with the thirty pieces of silver.

This betrayal leads us to look at the buying-selling relationship as a whole. If this relationship is dangerous, it is not only because of the intrinsic, supreme value of the human person. It is necessary to protect us from money because of the value we receive from Jesus Christ.

And so that we can understand the nature and can measure the intensity of the bond he establishes with each person, Jesus Christ himself submitted to this condition and became a purchased object to show us clearly that there is no other possibility, that all subjection of men and women to money is eminently serious.

The selling of Jesus, first foreshadowed by the story of Joseph sold by his brothers, then by Amos (2:6), shows the constancy of the selling relationship and carries its meaning to the absolute. This sale defines all selling. "They sold the Righteous." This act, which is our act, is reflected in each selling relationship. Now all money affairs are characterized by the fact that Jesus became the object of a money relationship. And because the Son of God was thus turned into merchandise, all subordination of humankind to money is intolerable.

This subordination is not necessarily restricted to the sale of slaves or the labor force. It occurs in each selling transaction, which inevitably sets up a destructive, competitive relationship even when the sale is of an ordinary object. In every case, one person is trying to establish superiority over another. The idea that selling can be a service is false; in truth the only thing expressed by the transaction is a will to power, a wish to subordinate life to money.

The selling relationship, moreover, has another characteristic, deriving from what we have already said: it profanes that which is sacred. The prophecy of Ezekiel about Tyre strongly and clearly reveals that commerce ends up by profaning the sanctuary. After having described at length Tyre's imports and exports, all its trade which leads to power (chapters 26—27), Ezekiel concludes: "By the multitude of your iniquities, in the unrighteousness of your trade you *profaned* your sanctuaries" (Ezek 28:18). We well know, in the last analysis, what this profanation of what God has chosen for himself means and where it leads. But this verse (along with the rest of the teaching about selling) also explains Jesus' reaction against the moneychangers in the Temple. Certainly this was no moralistic reaction against a more or less honest commerce. It was Jesus' revulsion against the profaners of the Temple, those who brought business into the place where God's grace should be manifest, and the many others who by their presence alone prophesied the supreme profanation of God's work which would soon be accomplished at the hands of Judas.

The selling relationship helps us better understand the whole Hebrew law, which in fact is concerned with protecting human life from the aggression of money. Money is a force that is destructive to life, and the Old Testament's fragmentary provisions witness to God's sovereignty over life against this aggressive force. They suggest that the first limitation on the role of money is human life.

But money's attack is not only exterior. Human life is at risk not only in the power struggle that money provokes. Money brings another familiar idea into play: temptation. The power of money is always actively tempting us. We must guard against thinking that this temptation is only a movement of our heart toward an object we desire to possess, for example, money. It is not only our nature that tempts us when we are in the presence of money. Of course the temptation to wealth exists; in chapter two we analyzed the human face of this temptation and said that all we have to do to be lost in riches is to follow our own heart. But the situation goes beyond human nature, for this temptation involves possession by a spirit different from the Spirit of God. Money is only the material sign of inner possession. It is the channel and means, but its force would not be so formidable if it were not accompanied by this spirit and used by this power which seeks to seduce us, to possess us, to make us live apart from God, and ultimately to win our love.

Possession by this power is broadly characterized by the general consensus which gives money effective social and political power in every human society. Money has no material force except as people attribute force to it. Money as an object is not the master of states, of armies, of the masses or of the mind except by humanity's consent to its authority. And it is possible to speak of laws of money only to the extent that people are willing to comply with them. Money would be nothing, materially speaking, without human consent.

It is a strange sort of convention which leads people to attribute, both by judgment and by will, value to something which in itself has no value of use or of exchange.

This is completely unexplainable and irrational. Nothing, whether in human nature or in the nature of things, whether in technology or in reason, adequately explains the original act of creating and accepting money. Nothing explains the blind confidence that we continue, in spite of all crises, to place in money. This is an absurdity which neither economists nor sociologists are able to clarify. The collective attitude of all humankind, this consensus, this submission, are incomprehensible if they are not traced back to the spiritual power of money. If money is not a spiritual power which invades us, enslaving our hearts and minds, replacing God's spirit in us, then our behavior is simply absurd. If people everywhere place such importance on the symbol of money, it is because they have already been seduced and internally possessed by the spirit of money.

In order to keep us from thinking we can remain independent of this power, the Bible gives three examples of this possession.

First, the first priest, Aaron, the first to offer sacrifices (Lev 9), the father of priests (Lev 21), was also the person who built the golden calf for his people. Substituting the worship of the golden idol for the worship of God, he showed his change of guiding spirit.

Second, the greatest king, Solomon, was attracted to false gods by his foreign wives and was likewise seduced by money. The close connection between the two temptations is made particularly clear in Deuteronomy 17:17—the king must have neither too many wives nor too much money. Samuel had warned the people that the king would take over their wealth, that he would be particularly overcome by the power of money. Moreover it was certainly the spirit of money that brought about the fulfillment of God's word of condemnation against Solomon: his son wished to impose the same heavy yoke—that is, the same taxes—on the people, and we know that for this reason the unity of Israel was broken (see 1 Sam 8; 1 Kings 10—12).

Finally, the prophets were seduced by the spirit of money and spoke according to this spirit rather than by the Word of God. This is more than a simple corruption of mankind; it is a falsification of God's Word by the adoption of another spirit (Mic 3:11). We know about Balaam's debate when he was called to prophesy for money (Num 22—23). Thus Scripture shows us that it is possible for the priest, the king and the prophet to be seduced by the spirit of money, even though not only their duties but also their vocation as types of Jesus Christ should have protected them from this.

Jesus was only the object of the power of money. He was never possessed by it. But the types of Jesus (prophet, priest and king) were able to be possessed by it. Even they are subject to the universal human condition characterized by submission to the power of money.

And when this seductive power succeeds in arousing love in the human heart, it shows plainly that it is a spiritual force and that its meaning does not stop with exterior acts but involves all human destiny.

Love God or Love Mammon. Although it is possible to say, following biblical guidelines, that the conflict is ultimately a conflict of love, a decision to love either God or money, we must be careful not to take *love* to mean a rather vague sentiment, a more or less valid passion, in any case a limited relationship. In reality love, in the Bible, is utterly totalitarian. It comes from the entire person; it involves the whole person and binds the whole person without distinction. Love reaches down into the roots of human beings and does not leave them intact. It leads to identification and assimilation between the lover and the beloved. Jesus Christ teaches us in great detail that our love binds us to the spiritual future of our beloved. This is how we must understand the connection between Christians and Christ, which is a love relationship. Love led Christ to follow us in our entire condition, but inversely, today it joins us to Christ in everything—his life, his death, his resurrection and his glory. Where Christ is, there also is the one who loves Christ. Such is the force, the vigor, of this bond.

Love for money is not a lesser relationship. By this love, we join ourselves to money's fate. "For where your treasure is, there will your heart be also" (Mt 6:21).

Ultimately, we follow what we have loved most intensely either into eternity or into death. To love money is to be condemned to follow it in its destruction, its disappearance, its annihilation and its death. It is thus extremely important that we never try to justify, however little, an attachment to money or the importance we attribute to it. Nowhere are Christians told that their love for money justifies it or causes it to be used to God's glory or elevates it toward the Good. The exact opposite is said: that our attachment to money pushes us with it headlong into nothingness.

To the extent that biblical love is totalitarian, it cannot stand sharing. We cannot have two spiritual lives; we cannot be divided. We cannot "halt between two opinions"; we can neither serve nor love two masters. Because love makes us follow the beloved and nothing else, we cannot love two things at the same time. Jesus firmly points out the necessity of choosing. "He will hate the one, and love the other." To love one is not simply to be unacquainted with or indifferent to the other; it is *to hate the other.*

Do we really believe that if money were only an object with no spiritual significance Jesus would have gone that far?

To love money, to be attached to it, is to hate God. We can now understand why St. Paul says that "the love of money is the root of all evils" (1 Tim 6:10). This is not a hackneyed bit of popular morality. It is an accurate summary of this conflict. Insofar as the love of money is hatred for God, it certainly is a root of all the evils that accompany separation from God. And in this same text Paul stressed that those who are possessed by this love have lost the faith: it comes to exactly the same thing. But a person does not lose the faith over a simple moral error. It is always Satan's seduction that causes people to wander away from the faith.

But we are so used to minimizing the content of revelation that we think all of this is well within our reach. When we say that everything boils down to love, we feel very comfortable again, for we think that nothing could be easier. And we are tempted to say, "As long as we don't love money, everything will fall into place," or even to affirm, "I don't love money." Perhaps many Christians say this in good faith. But we must remember first the depth of this "bond of love," a depth which is beyond our reach, then that the love of money is aroused and provoked by its spiritual power.

Therefore, even if to some extent we are able to master our thoughts and emotions and thus the inclinations which come from our hearts alone, we still cannot dominate the love of money, for this is aroused by a seductive power which is far beyond us, just as it is maintained by a force that is outside us. This is what Paul reminds us of (and he is speaking about more than the power of money) when he teaches that "we are not contending against flesh and blood, but against the principalities, against the powers, against the world rulers of this present darkness" (Eph 6:12). It is thus not within our abilities to get rid of this love. When we are caught (as we all are), our force is insufficient. God's intervention is necessary.

Judgment and Deliverance. But here again we must be careful not to oversimplify things. When God attacks this power that has us in its grip because it has aroused our love, when he tears away the treasure to which we have become attached, he is attacking us. God's deliverance is not a stroke of a magic wand which leaves us intact, the way we were. It is a rescue of part of ourselves. Consequently we may have the impression, the feeling, of being amputated, diminished. God, who is delivering us from the shackles of this power, is also destroying its roots which have taken hold of us. He saves us but, St. Paul says, "only as through fire" (1 Cor 3:15), for he is destroying whatever does not resist this fire.

This deliverance results from passing through God's judgment, and it bears fruit when we accept this judgment. The first judgment is of Mammon itself. For it is one of the conquered, deposed powers which Christ, by dying on the cross, has stripped of authority. Mammon is judged; its capacity and the length of its reign have been reduced. But it retains a strength which is far greater than ours. It has terrible power, as we often observe.

Nevertheless, because of this judgment against Mammon, our judgment can be one of liberation. Because Mammon has been judged, when God judges us he liberates us from Mammon. Without this, the judgment would clearly show that we belong to Satan with no hope of appeal.

God's judgment is not only on our person but also on our possessions and actions. Thus it is judgment on our treasure, on all aspects of our money. We cannot avoid this test.

This is described in Ezekiel 27—28. There man is on trial because of his wealth and the power which has given him money, but also because of all the effects this money has had on his heart. The will to dominate, pride, the need for security, autonomy before God—these are all condemned at the same time.

This is the same judgment that we find in Jesus' word to the rich young man. This man does what is right and has no need to feel guilty about his moral behavior. Even with his money he does what he can. There is, however, one thing out of place: his relationship to his money. He can of course use it morally; that solves nothing. He remains bound to this power, and Jesus shows him his real situation. We know that we must not make a general ethical principle out of Jesus' command and affirm that every Christian must sell all his goods. But even if this is not the meaning of his command, we all still must accept it as a judgment, a revelation of our real love for money despite our claim to be free of this. As long as we have not heard this judgment, we are not free. As long as we have not measured our lives against this specific order from God, we are still possessed by money. And when we have heard this judgment, then like the rich young man we can leave, head bowed, conquered but perhaps delivered.

Delivered and not condemned. What is condemned here is the power of money and not the man. For we must always remember that God's judgment is not *against* us but *for* us. God has neither the will nor the intention to destroy and condemn us; he wants to save us and make us live. This judgment therefore is not made in order to damn us, and the command is not given to the young man to show how wicked he is and how right God would be to condemn him. On the contrary, its intention is to show that he is weak, a slave; that money is a power; that man's strength is unable to free him; that he needs Jesus' intervention and grace. No other way out is possible. It is useless to try to avoid passing through judgment.

The very character of this judgment (which we will examine later) introduces us to a world that is different from the natural world. It leads us into God's world which, already on earth, is characterized by grace. We must think again of the impact of this overused word. Grace is God's action, freely willed and *given without cost*. Indeed the major characteristic of God's world is the fact that in it everything is given freely. Grace is grace precisely because it is not bought. "Ho, every one who thirsts, come to the waters; and he who has no money, come, buy and eat! Come, buy wine and milk without money and without price" (Is 55:1). We are looking at God's extraordinary generosity which means, on the one hand, that we would never be able to pay an adequate price, whatever we brought, to buy God's pardon; and, on the other hand, that God does not obey the world's law but another law, the law of giving. God's one way of acting is giving. Only once did God submit to the law of selling. He allowed his Son to be sold. He agreed to pay the price of our redemption. Redemption is very literally the payment of Satan's price in order to free us.

God agrees to go beyond the world of giving to deal with Satan, and there again we must measure the depth of God's love. He gives up his own will to accept the enemy's law, just as in Christ he accepts the needs and limitations of flesh and blood.

God pays a price. He accepts the exchange that Satan demanded, and Satan can claim to have put God under his own law, the law of selling.

But when God thus lowers himself, he becomes Incarnate. This is the act by which he enters into the human condition in order to liberate us from our sinful state. And we are ultimately led to another act of grace. God pays the price so that he can give freedom and act in grace. "You were bought with a price" (1 Cor 6:20; 7:23). Indeed no price can be higher than that one. We must constantly remind ourselves of the high value God must place on each of our lives to thus give up his Son. This reminder is a basic principle of the Christian life: God redeems you and liberates you to live a free life. God puts an enormously high price on you. God has paid this price. These three aspects of a single reality have results which, though easy to see, have great importance in everyday life.

But when God thus binds himself to the law of selling and agrees to pay the price, he freely *gives* his Son in order to *give* liberty; we are brought right back to giving. God's only way of acting is giving. As he gave life, so he gave his Son. As his Son gave his life ("No one takes it from me, but I lay it down of my own accord"—Jn 10:18), so God gave pardon—and this is grace. In this new world we are entering, nothing is for sale; everything is given away. The mark of the world of money (where all is bought, where selling with all its consequences is the normal way to act) is the exact opposite of the mark of God's world where everything is free, where giving is the normal way to act. This is indeed different from our usual way of acting. This behavior is dictated by grace. Likewise the love created by money and by selling is the exact opposite of the love created by grace and by giving. Their direction is different, as Anders Nygren points out in *Agape and Eros*.

For Mammon's work is the exact opposite of God's work. Given this opposition, we understand why Jesus demands a choice between Mammon and God. He is not speaking of just any other power, just any other god; he is speaking of the one who goes directly against God's action, the one who makes "nongrace" reign in the world. Of course any other power and any other god is in a sense God's opposite, but none is more opposite than Mammon from the standpoint of behavior. For Mammon is unable to be more or less in agreement with grace. It loses all reason for existence, all power over us, as soon as grace enters our heart.

The Futility of Conciliation. We are always trying to bring about, one way or another, a conciliation of the two, but it is out of the question. The parable of the unforgiving servant shows this. When he had received grace (remission of his debt, renunciation of the creditor's rights), this debtor entered the world of grace. This assumed a new behavior on his part: mercy expressed in giving. If we refuse grace for others, we refuse it for ourselves also, which means that we have not yet entered the world of grace.

This helps us understand the danger in the Catholic doctrine of merit. Merit earned by means of works and virtues is a way of paying God, of buying his grace. In other words, the merit system tries to make the law of money penetrate God's work, to introduce Mammon into the world of grace. By doing this it destroys the whole work of God. Nothing is left but the law of our world, and money is truly king. The sale of indulgences for money was not an incidental distortion; it was the logical result of the doctrine that grace can be bought by works.[1]

This is the error that makes us imagine, as we so often do, that God's judgment is a weighing of good and of evil, of good works and of sins. How often we think that God's judgment is based on a weighing (the scale is a symbol of justice) or a balance sheet! At the end of the big book where all our good and bad deeds are recorded, the Great Bookkeeper tallies up the balance.

But God is neither a bookkeeper nor a grocer weighing merchandise in order to set its price. To think of judgment this way is, once again, to make the law of money penetrate God's truth. It is once again to obey the order of buying and selling, which God's world does not obey. God's judgment is a judgment of grace. Because God's gift in his Son is free, the whole perspective changes, and we have no right to want an accounting system. This would be fatal for us. But mercy triumphs over judgment (Jas 2:12-13), and we understand why God's judgment on us and on our money (at the same time as on our works) ultimately introduces us into the world of grace.

---

[1]Only one text seems to go against all this: the parable of the kingdom of heaven where the man sells all he has to buy the field where the treasure, symbolizing the kingdom, is found (Mt 13:44). But we must note first of all that this is a parable, and therefore we must not turn the behavior described there into an example to follow when this behavior is not itself the point of the parable. The parable of the talents is not an invitation to invest our money and make it increase! We know that we must look for *one* teaching in the parable (and not a multitude of teachings). This will be expressed in the kernel, the point, of the story, but not in its details. Here the meaning is not about selling but about giving up everything one has for the kingdom of heaven.

The second observation is that this text is parallel to verse 45 which describes God's act in giving up his Son to liberate humankind. Finally, in any case, it has to do with the kingdom of heaven, in other words, as Cullmann shows, with a splendor that is inserted into the context of the world. This is surely what the text means when it speaks of the purchase of the *field* (and not of the treasure). It is the context, and not the kingdom of heaven itself, which is submitted to the law of selling.

Already in the Old Testament, in the middle of the promises of wealth as a blessing, we have a sign of this free grace, right at the heart of God's people. This sign is the Levites, men who owned nothing, neither lands nor money. When the land of Israel was divided among the tribes, nothing was given to the children of Levi. Nor were they allowed to have personal income. This arrangement was intended to assure the freedom of the priesthood, the possibility of conducting worship anywhere without hindrances, for the Levite had to be able to move anywhere without being impeded by tribal boundaries. Even more, it was intended to be an evidence in the midst of the people of God's gift to them, of the fact that God's act was free and without charge. "And the LORD said to Aaron, 'You shall have no inheritance in their land, neither shall you have any portion among them; I am your portion and your inheritance among the people of Israel' " (Num 18:20).

The Levites are evidence that God gives life freely. For they live entirely from the income of the altar, a part of the tithe and offerings. They live in relation to God, from what is given to God and what God gives them. They are evidence that God liberates (as he did in Egypt) without charge, for they are free of political and social rules.

They are evidence that God reveals himself without charge, for their priestly function is God's gift to Israel: "I give your priesthood as a gift" (Num 18:7). But they are also evidence that God is master of all things, owns all things and uses them as he pleases, for the Levite is at home everywhere and collects tithes from everyone. They are thus evidence of God's grace by their presence alone, by their unique situation in the midst of a people who were soon going to give in to the lure of money, possession and stability.

Money as a Test

"And he sat down opposite the treasury, and watched the multitude putting money into the treasury" (Mk 12:41). Jesus' attention to people giving their offerings calls us also to look at giving. Jesus did not just happen to be watching. It was no accident that he noticed the poor woman putting in a few coins as her offering. Jesus was acting intentionally. He sat in front of the treasury—the offering box—in order to see. He watched people giving. And it was not the amount they gave that interested him but the way they gave. This shows that Jesus paid close attention to the money question. He spoke of it often, and here we see that in money matters, no behavior escapes Jesus' observation. We must not deceive ourselves: our honesty and generosity are not being questioned, but how we give. Even if Jesus does not make a negative judgment here, we know by the positive judgment he expresses that he is judging. This implies then that we must pass under Jesus' scrutiny each time we handle money. He sat there on purpose. Our attitude toward money becomes a sort of criterion.

We can speak of a "money test." If our attitude toward money is extremely important, it is not only because money plays an enormous role in society. Here again the Bible tells us that with regard to money, our lives must answer a question that may be decisive. The money test shows whether we have truly understood grace. Our actions regarding money are important inasmuch as they are decisions and spiritual acts. Material acts are minor things, consequences, although in reality these consequences are necessary and inevitable.

That money can be a test, a touchstone in Christian life, is particularly clear in the story of the unjust steward as told in Luke 16:1-13:

There was a rich man who had a steward, and charges were brought to him that this man was wasting his goods. And he called him and said to him, "What is this that I hear about you? Turn in the account of your stewardship, for you can no longer be steward." And the steward said to himself, "What shall I do, since my master is taking the stewardship away from me? I am not strong enough to dig, and I am ashamed to beg. I have decided what to do, so that people may receive me into their houses when I am put out of the stewardship." So, summoning his master's debtors one by one, he said to the first,

"How much do you owe my master?" He said, "A hundred measures of oil." And he said to him, "Take your bill, and sit down quickly and write fifty." Then he said to another, "And how much do you owe?" He said, "A hundred measures of wheat." He said to him, "Take your bill, and write eighty." The master commended the dishonest steward for his shrewdness; for the sons of this world are more shrewd in dealing with their own generation than the sons of light. And I tell you, make friends for yourselves by means of unrighteous mammon, so that when it fails they may receive you into the eternal habitations.

He who is faithful in a very little is faithful also in much; and he who is dishonest in a very little is dishonest also in much. If then you have not been faithful in the unrighteous mammon, who will entrust to you the true riches? And if you have not been faithful in that which is another's, who will give you that which is your own? No servant can serve two masters; for either he will hate the one and love the other, or he will be devoted to the one and despise the other. You cannot serve God and mammon.

It seems to me first of all that this passage forms a whole. The parable of the unjust steward cannot be separated, just because it is a story, from the explanations attached to it (verses 9-13). The fact that the saying about Mammon is found in another context in the Gospel according to St. Matthew does not mean that we should dissociate the teaching given in verses 9-13 from the story itself. Contrary to those authors who think these are unrelated pericopes, I think there are very strong links between them. For those who separate the two elements, the only conclusion of the parable is that "the sons of this world are more shrewd."

Now we must note that this parable is included in a whole collection of parables about wealth: Luke 15:11-32, the prodigal son; 16:14-18, the Pharisees who were lovers of money; 16:19-31, the rich man and Lazarus. It would be surprising if this parable, which directly evokes the problem of money, did not include any teaching about the question since it is part of this collection. And this text would say nothing about money if verse 8 were its only conclusion, its punchline.

Moreover, we would wonder where verses 9-12 fit in. They are not closely linked with verse 13; we do not find them in the synoptics in any other context. These are isolated sayings, hard to explain by themselves. But in order to separate them, we would have to assume that the first words of verse 9 ("And I tell you, make friends for yourselves...") are an interpolation. As a matter of fact, these words point to a clear connection with the parable: *This is what the master says* in the parable, *and I tell you* ... The "make friends for yourselves" corresponds exactly to the steward's concerns.

Finally, verse 13 should also be seen as part of the story, as Martin Achard emphasizes, because of the word play between *Mammon* and *'Aman* (the authentic *amen*) which was in the Aramaic account but which the Greek translation evidently got rid of.[2] The story of the steward evokes the conflict between two masters who struggle for his trust, and Jesus responds to this with the saying reported in verse 13.

There is therefore a real unity in this passage. Verses 9-13 make up the true explanation of the parable in which verse 8 is only an incident, almost parenthetical. This explanation is important for understanding Jesus' teaching about money. For we must note that the meaning of all the verses turns around the word translated "unrighteous mammon," which is, more precisely, "the mammon of iniquity." Now if Luke, who tended to be hellenistic, keeps this Aramaic term rather than using the corresponding Greek words, it is because this term has a force, a value which no other term can translate. We see the reality of this when we speak of the power of money.

---

[2]Following the etymology of *Mammon* which Martin Achard adopts from Hauck, *'Aman* is a root which implies a sense of stability, of firmness. From this root are derived terms meaning "to be faithful" or "to trust," "to be stable" or "to endure," and "to believe," as well as "truth" and "faithfulness." Thus Jesus' parable contains a series of word plays on Mammon and Amen: the power of wealth, faithfulness and faith. Mammon therefore is presented as something solid, a stable power demanding trust and faith.

Characteristics of Mammon. What are the characteristics of this Mammon?[3] He is, in the first place, "of iniquity." In other words, nothing in him could conform either to human righteousness or, especially, to God's righteousness. Once again we leave the area of morality. If we were discussing wealth (money which man has accumulated and earned), we would not always consider it unrighteous (from a moral point of view). Some riches have been honestly earned. We could then restrict the teaching to unrighteous or unjust wealth. This would allow us to dispose of the text easily. But this is not the case: iniquity is a necessary attribute of Mammon and is characteristic of all his aspects. This means both that Mammon generates and provokes iniquity and that Mammon, symbol of unrighteousness, emanates from iniquity. In any case, unrighteousness, the antithesis of God's word, is Mammon's trademark.

Furthermore, Mammon is one of the "little things" mentioned in verse 10. The opposition between God and Mammon is no manichean dualism. Mammon is not an anti-God. He is certainly God's opposite in the area of behavior, but he enjoys no equality with God. He is nothing but a defeated power, nothing but an object in the hands of Almighty God who does as he wishes with him and who leaves him a little time because in his patience he leaves everyone a little time. It is not appropriate to pull up the tares with the wheat before the time of the harvest.

Next, Mammon is a liar. This is another part of his iniquity, for he is opposed to true wealth (verse 11), or rather truthful wealth, wealth which is in the truth. He belongs to the world of darkness, and he leads us into the darkness and holds us there by the power of lies. In the biblical perspective, Mammon shows himself to be a lying power by constantly deceiving us. He arouses desires which he never satisfies.

"He who loves money will not be satisfied with money; nor he who

---

[3]Some of the observations that follow were inspired by J. Kressmann, *Le piège du Dieu vivant* [The trap of the living God], and by Martin Achard, "Notes sur Mammon" [Notes on Mammon] *Etudes Théologiques,* 1953.

loves wealth, with gain" (Eccles 5:10). Mammon's force permits him to possess his worshipers. We see Mammon's work in half-tones: it is a counterfeit of God's work, with belief, hope, justification and love. But this is all a falsification of faith, hope, justice and charity. "By definition Mammon is wealth that is not enjoyed. For enjoyment is itself a grace—and Mammon and all grace are mutually exclusive" (J. Kressmann).

When money seems to be fulfilling the one who loves money, the ground he meant to fortify slips out from under his feet. Mammon strips the rich of their very lives, even while giving them more money. He deceives us by trying to pass for something stable, for real solidity, for that which merits trust. This confusion, revealed by his very name, implies that he appeals to our faith by giving us guarantees, when Mammon is really nothing more than emptiness and illusion.

Finally, Mammon belongs to another. This reminds us that our money belongs to another: to Mammon. And he also belongs to someone else; he belongs to Satan. An amazing observation in the epistle of James is fully realized in the area of money: "You covet and cannot obtain" (Jas 4:2). A person never ultimately possesses money, for it always belongs to another. It flees from our hands, for it does not depend on us. Another master commands it. But this master seeks to reestablish unity. By using money as a channel, he seeks to take possession of man and become his master. In the parable of the unjust steward, Jesus is speaking to those who belong to God ("the disciples," verse 1). Henceforth for them money will always be a foreign value; it always belongs to another, for they do not belong to its master.

Thus is Mammon characterized by these verses, which raise the question of fidelity. To be faithful is to follow the law and the will of one's master. Here we have two possible masters: Mammon and God. Each has his own law, and each has his own will. There are therefore two possible ways of being faithful and obedient.

The two masters establish two systems of behavior, love and value, two opposite laws. We can therefore be faithful to one master by following his law, but not to the other. We can be very faithful to Mammon by being conscientious stewards of the goods and riches of the world, by making them multiply according to the law of money, by playing the economic or political game. But then we must not seek out the spiritual reality of this game. At most we accommodate ourselves (and in truth, quite well) to a type of morality.

Or we can be faithful to God, having our homeland not on earth but in Christ, seeking God's will, trying to live by his grace, but we must recognize that this leads to an obvious ignorance of economic life in the world of money. Now this double loyalty does not cause great difficulties when the questions are kept strictly separated, when a person who lives in the world is ignorant of God's will or when a Christian is shut up in a monastery to avoid touching filthy Mammon. (But in this case the administrators of the monastery themselves have the problem that the brothers are able to avoid.) But Jesus does not think such a separation is ideal or even just. Rather the Christian must use money (and the economic world as well), however unjust it may be, however alienated it may be, and, from the viewpoint of an intense faith, however unimportant it may be.

We must use what Mammon offers. We must neither neglect it nor refuse it. But all the difficulty is in the *how?* And here we find the point of this teaching. When we enter Mammon's territory, when we receive money, his channel of power, when we are involved in buying and selling, are we going to obey the law of money, are we going to continue the circle of mutual sales, in other words, are we going to adopt allegiance to Mammon? The very thing Jesus asks here is that we maintain our allegiance to God. This faithfulness to God is not reserved for spiritual things; it must be engraved on the things of the world.

Allegiance to God must penetrate the world of money. When we enter this world, we must be attached to Jesus Christ in order not to adopt its law, just as Christ, when he entered our world, did not adopt the law of sin even though it is inscribed in human flesh.

Here then we have two worlds, one of selling and one of giving, totally opposed to each other and therefore strangers and without communication with each other. Jesus asks us to penetrate the world of selling in order to penetrate it with grace by our faithfulness to God, the only Master. This is just the reverse of the situation we described earlier, when we spoke of those Christians who obey the law of selling in their lives and thoughts, even of God himself, and who make this law penetrate the world of grace.

Here, to the contrary, grace must use the very instruments that are customary in the world of selling. Grace must invade the power of money, for when Mammon is destroyed by grace, it is no longer a formidable power.

This is why we must be faithful to God in those things which belong to another. Above the master who appears to be giving us our money stands the real Master, to whom alone we owe allegiance. He entrusts us with a particular work to do in this world. We must therefore, by the intervention of grace, break the chain of buying and selling and the law of money which is enslaving humankind.

A Picture of Grace. Now the unjust steward of the parable is given to us as an example in several ways. We will look at only one. Even in his dishonesty itself (which is not praised) he accomplishes one of those amazing acts representative of grace: he releases debtors from their debts. Of course he does it with someone else's money (as we must always do, because when we pardon we are using God's pardon), but the important thing is that his action is without charge. It destroys the debtor's obligation. His generous act, so open to criticism from many points of view, has the distinction of making debtors enter the world of pardon, of giving, of remission of debt, ultimately of grace. In this, the steward who is unfaithful to money is faithful to grace. Thus these men that he brings into the world of grace become his friends, for this is how the giving relationship operates. And of course from now on they will receive him in their new home, here called the "eternal habitations," or, to be precise, the throne where God's great grace presides.

This shows us what sort of test money is. The steward in the parable is called "the steward of iniquity." This is often translated as "unfaithful steward," which takes away the whole impact and the entire meaning of the expression. In reality, this parable is about a steward who must supervise iniquitous and unjust things. And this is what we are all called to do on earth. When we have been able to remain faithful to our Lord in unjust things, then he who has true riches at his disposal, riches which do not perish, entrusts us with them because he knows that under our management faithfulness will be preserved. Now these goods are too important (they are the things of the kingdom) to give to just anybody ("do not throw your pearls before swine"). It is important to be sure of the ability of the one who will receive these goods. But this ability is, above all, respect for the Master's will. There is no better way to discover this than by the simple money test.

We must not hope to get out of this test by being pious, moral or even believing. In reality God's riches are entrusted only to the person who knows how to remain faithful to God in the midst of Mammon riches. Such a person does not think money is unimportant, that it is not a question worth discussing among Christians, that material things mean nothing. Nor does such a person divide his life in two, with two loyalties. To the first group our text says that if a person is not faithful in small things, he will not receive big ones; to the second group it says that a person *cannot* serve two masters.

This explanation of the parable of the steward allows us to resolve an apparent contradiction. Although riches belong to God and come from God, here we are told very clearly that money, called Mammon, belongs to Satan and comes from Satan.

The contradiction is only apparent, for when God affirms his sovereignty over riches, a sovereignty which will appear in the heavenly Jerusalem, he is speaking to faith. On the one hand, he affirms to us an eternal but hidden reality; on the other hand, he asks us to recognize his sovereignty in the world, to manifest it, to ascribe riches to him. This is possible only by faith.

In the material reality of the fallen world, however, where men and women are fallen, sinful and in revolt, money is effectively a rebel power of seduction and death belonging to Satan. The same apparent contradiction operates in the realm of the state: on the one hand, "there is no authority except from God" (Rom 13:1); on the other, the state is the beast which ascends from the bottomless pit (Rev 17:8).

This contradiction is resolved in the eschatological perspective and in the action the Christian—and only the Christian—is called to take in the world: the action of being faithful to God in the world, using the instruments of revolt and of evil.

This attitude toward money is essential. On it ultimately depends, not salvation, but the assignment of the kingdom's riches to manage for God. These riches, we are told, are already ours (and it is true that by faith we are already heirs of the kingdom and joint heirs with Christ), but simple ownership does not guarantee proper usage. God gives these riches only to those capable of managing them.

Money in Christian Life

What behavior then is required by our faithfulness? This is really the whole problem of our attitude toward money, whose underlying principles we have already discovered in the parable of the steward of iniquity. We are asked to make free grace penetrate the world of selling, liabilities, compensation, competition. But how can this be done? The Bible again gives us numerous directives, which we must not turn into laws.

Side with Humanity against Money. First, in the competition that always exists, as we have seen, between man and money, we must always side with humanity against the power of money. This power wants to destroy us. In our money dealings with others, money pushes us to put its interests (which we assimilate as our own interests) before those of the person with whom we are doing business. Scripture tells us how we must choose: we must decide in favor of the person and against money.

In this area Mosaic legislation is particularly abundant, and we will look at it as an example. When we are lending money, when we find ourselves in a creditor-debtor relationship, this legislation teaches us not to behave like a real creditor according to the laws of money.[4] If we retain the traditional schema of the poor and unfortunate debtor enslaved by the extreme need of money, the law of the old covenant clearly teaches us to respect the person rather than money. This is why lending with interest was prohibited. "If you lend money to any of my people with you who is poor, you shall not be to him as a creditor, and you shall not exact interest from him" (Ex 22:25; see also Lev 25:35-38). Interest taken on money is a typical example of the type of money relationship where the debtor is scorned, disdained or ignored. Two elements need to be stressed in these texts.

First, there is a difference between the Israelite to whom one must lend without interest and the foreigner to whom it is permissible to lend with interest (Deut 23:20). We must not think that this expresses contempt for the Gentiles or that it permits them to be shamelessly exploited, destroyed because they are not really human, or subjected to Israel. Neither must we think that this refers to two different levels of civilization. In reality, there is a spiritual meaning in this contradiction. As a matter of fact the foreigner residing in Israel (who would consequently be very easy to oppress), an easy mark for a loan with interest, is to be treated like an Israelite. Only the foreigner *who lives far away* can be exploited. This implies a difference based on proximity. The person who is near you, the one who lives with you (Lev 25:35-36), the one who is of your people (Ex 22:25)—for these people there is to be no extortion, no interest, no law of money. We know what this proximity implies:

---

[4]This is true only if this relationship conforms to the ancient reality of the superiority of the creditor. Obviously in our society, the debtor is often much more powerful than the creditor. The corporation cannot be compared with the hundreds of shareholders who compose it.

a neighbor-to-neighbor relationship.

Thus we are being taught that in our relations with our neighbors the law of money must stay in the background. This implies that we must abandon the impersonal attitude which treats all business contacts as strangers. We must instead make the money relationship secondary in order to establish proximity. When we see someone as our neighbor, he is once again fully human, an individual, a person to whom we are responsible.

The second element to remember is found in Leviticus 25. The passage which prohibits interest ends with the reminder that God led the people of Israel out of Egypt and gave them Canaan (verse 38). This reminder has to do with the fact that the relations God establishes among men are based on grace and are without charge. God gave freedom to his people. He gave them a country. He thus made grace enter the world; he introduced the law of giving. And by reminding them of his gift, God can demand that Israel likewise live by giving, that the people no longer obey the law of money (which has vested interests) but the law of grace. And this is confirmed by Jesus Christ: "You received without paying, give without pay" (Mt 10:8), even to the point of lending without interest. The link between the two motifs is perfectly clear.

We find another indication that the creditor is called to give priority to human life in the legislation about pledges. The law has much to say about taking pledges by force: do not take clothing unless you give it back before sundown, do not take the upper millstone, etc. (Ex 22:26; Deut 24:6-13). Indeed the debtor is to be allowed to keep everything necessary for living. The money relationship must not lead the debtor to lack what is necessary for his material life. It must not even be the occasion for an invasion of the debtor's privacy to intimidate him; it is forbidden to enter a house to take a pledge. Moreover the whole system of pledges is looked down on, for it is a relationship of violence, of constraint, of defiance. The recommended relationship, by contrast, is one of trust, for defiance destroys man. And too bad if the creditor is not reimbursed; better that than to overburden the debtor's life and to corrupt the relations between two people. These regulations constantly remind us that we have to choose between our money and the other person's life. It is not possible to reconcile the two.

The same life-protecting attitude dictates the biblical commands about wages. Here again we are looking at a money relationship, and the person who pays the wages is the superior because of money. The employer has not only the hired workers' work at his disposal, but—what is more important, the Bible indirectly reminds us—their lives. One's money is the direct means of dominating and destroying others.

"You shall not oppress a hired servant who is poor and needy, whether he is one of your brethren or one of the sojourners who are in your land within your towns; you shall give him his hire on the day he earns it, before the sun goes down (for he is poor, and sets his heart upon it)" (Deut 24:14-15). "Woe to him . . . who makes his neighbor serve him for nothing, and does not give him his wages" (Jer 22:13). "Behold, the wages of the laborers . . . which you kept back by fraud, cry out" (Jas 5:4). These texts, among others, make the following points. First, in the superior position given to money in the labor contract, there is a threat, there is temptation to oppress. Here again we find the theme of proximity discussed above: a person must come to the point of considering workers as neighbors and consequently of somehow drowning in friendship the exclusive juridical and economic labor contract, which wrongly absorbs the whole person. While now the labor contract subordinates the whole person to an employer, the situation must be completely reversed. The full human (and better yet, spiritual) relation of proximity, of neighbor to neighbor, must surround the labor contract. If the labor contract is subordinated to the neighbor-to-neighbor relationship, it will take on a new character.

Next, the worker must be paid his whole salary; that is, a sum that really corresponds with his production and not one that is more or less arbitrarily fixed in a more or less free contract where the boss (whether an individual or the state) holds the advantage. This implies the disappearance of profit. I cannot expand on that topic here; I mention it only as a guideline.

Finally, the texts remind us that wages must not be held back. This is a particularly dangerous type of pressure and exploitation. It can be done in several ways, such as paying wages in kind or settling with merchandise sold by the company store. Some might object that this is no longer done because of social legislation. This is only partly true. But the problem has existed, could reappear and still exists in many places.

Scripture insists that all these regulations have to do not with justice (not even social justice!) but with life. In all this, the boss can choose to be Mammon's instrument to crush the life of his workers, or he can choose not to. This is what James means when he says that the unpaid wages cry out to God: surely it is no accident that he uses the same phrase as Genesis speaking of Abel's blood which cries out from the ground to the Lord (Gen 4:10).

This explains the harshness of the punishment if man does not obey these regulations, if he ultimately chooses Mammon. Jeremiah, Malachi and James express the curse that is over this man. It is the most complete earthly rejection that can ever be expressed.

Do Not Love Money. The second aspect of Christian faithfulness in the world of money is the way we express the fact that we no longer love money. If Christians have accepted God's judgment delivering us from possession by the power of money, our spiritual reversal must not stay entirely within but must be expressed externally. If we really do not love money any longer, we must incarnate our new attitude.

Here again we will attempt to follow the Bible. But we must remember that we can speak only of attitudes that serve as *examples* and *signs*—that is, examples for all other related actions which the liberated Christian imagination can think of. These examples have no intrinsic or saving value; they simply point to the spiritual freedom of which God is the author.

We must not think of these examples as laws and obligations. Neither should we think that they are sufficient by themselves or that they express all justice.

The two attitudes given us by Scripture as expressions of the Christian's new situation are the rejection of savings and the absence of worry.

The rejection of savings. We must first consider what it means when a person puts money aside or insures himself (for the problem of insurance is included with the problem of savings: the two acts have the same meaning). Both these measures express the wish to take possession of the future, to guarantee oneself against whatever might happen —accidents, changes in job or financial standing. Sometimes a person is thinking of old age, sometimes of getting children established—in any case, it is a way to control the future. Facing the uncertainty of tomorrow, the risks of life, people put a stash aside to serve as a screen between themselves and reality. This is the way savings accounts work.

And for unbelievers, materialists, people in general, it is an absolutely legitimate thing to do. They cannot live with a totally risky future, thinking that the next second could upset their whole life and that they have no way to prevent this. The guarantee they need is provided by the accumulation of money. What shows how much we need security is our habit of rushing to obtain the guarantee of the state just as soon as the guarantee of money disappears (as it has in our time). Seen this way, state socialism is exactly the same as capitalist accumulation.

But starting with this search for security, savings lead very quickly to a will for autonomy. Those who possess much claim to be independent and say they are free. On this basis they wish to build their lives, orienting and directing them as they see best. As a result, this reinforces the bent of non-Christians, allowing them to swear that God is absent. "Soul, you have ample goods laid up for many years; take your ease, eat, drink, be merry" (Lk 12:19; see also 1 Tim 6:17-19).

But for those who have heard of God, and who have perhaps heard

God himself speaking, this attitude is much more serious. It implies actual defiance of God. It assumes either that God is incapable of correctly directing our lives, or that he has bad intentions toward us. If we are persuaded that God directs our lives (Ps 139), then to pile up savings is to refuse this direction, to protect ourselves against God's decisions concerning us. It then becomes an act that goes against God's free purposes with respect to us and against his free grace. This is how we seek to avoid uncertainty and indecision about our future.[5]

At this point all kinds of considerations intervene, coming sometimes from excellent theology and insisting first that God does not neglect human instruments for guiding life. Therefore savings accounts can be useful, and moreover it would be tempting God to want to count on his gifts alone. Second, it is possible to save money without putting one's trust in money, but only in God.

I think these objections are very ill founded. The best that can be said is that God directs our lives *in spite of* our precautions and savings accounts. Of course God uses human instruments, but that is no reason for *us* to accumulate instruments which have no meaning other than distrust of God. This is the enormous lesson of the prophets: if God is Israel's protector, Israel has no need to protect itself by treasonous alliances with Egypt or Babylon (Is 30 and 36, Jer 42, for example). It is exactly the same thing with savings accounts. For ultimately there is no way to share: either our confidence is in God or it is in our savings account. To claim that we can thus insure ourselves and still put our trust in God is to add hypocrisy to mistrust of God. For assuming that the only function of savings accounts is to assure our future, if we do not trust this means, why do we use it? That would be an insane thing to do. But in reality, what we call trust in God is only a word, and without daring to admit it, we really put our trust in money.

---

[5]We must remember that, in reality, the future is just as uncertain with savings as without them; but people, subjectively and in spite of all reasonable objections, hold on to the conviction that they are protected by money.

It goes without saying that this does not condemn all forms of saving. It does not condemn saving toward a specific objective (to give a gift, to buy a house to live in), and when we are involved in a business with very irregular income, it is normal to spread the earnings out over several years. The foresight of the peasant who saves seed for the following year is normal, as in industry are the indispensable savings for investment. But this only shows the limits of savings and insurance that are intended to guarantee the future of the individual or his children.

Now these savings show a very strange human trait. We distrust God and place our confidence in things. We prefer our relation to money over our relation to God. This money relationship is ultimately a subordination of what we are to what we have. Being thus entirely turned in on ourselves, we end up alienating ourselves in what we own. This is the dehumanization of the middle class.

We are called not to pile up savings, not to trust in this deceitful security (1 Tim 6:17-19), without however being essentially improvident and without giving in to foolish spending and waste. A biblical guideline must never become a way to justify our sin. The person who, whether improvident or a spendthrift by nature, does not save is not pronounced virtuous by Scripture; neither is he on right terms with the money question. For this person is almost fatally missing out on the positive side of this teaching, of which we will have more to say later.

Freedom from worry. All we have to do is remember the great passage in the Sermon on the Mount to realize what this freedom implies (Mt 6:25-34). Fortunately, the problem with worrying about money (and is that not our principal cause of worry?) is pointed out in this pericope to remind us that the spiritual question of money is not only for those who have money.

Mammon also attacks those who do not have money. The power of money subjects the poor as solidly as the rich. Some are subjected by their savings, others by their desire, worry, discontent—and everyone alike by covetousness.

Therefore the biblical teaching applies equally to all. Now, just as a savings account subjects people to what they possess, so worry enslaves them to what they do not have. Christ comes to announce liberation, emancipation, from this slavery.

Again, it must be understood that Jesus does not declare money worries unimportant. He does not call us to live only on the spiritual plane. He does not criticize the materialism of the person who has nothing. He does not say that we are wrong to be worried, because we ought to live in a carefree manner. He does not suggest evasion, and he does not judge us. He frees us, which is another thing altogether.

The liberation which Jesus brings about in us has a double foundation according to our text. First, we must *believe* that God actually knows we need material things in order to live. This is primarily a concrete and material evaluation of the existing situation, but it differs from the pagan response. Presented with this need, pagans worry about how to fulfill it. Christians put their trust in God, for God is truly concerned about these matters. They are not outside his grasp, and Jesus assures us that he will not let us be in want if we place our life in his hands.

It is nevertheless true that we see lots of people who do not have the necessities of life. The Bible teaches us that this may result from the fact that people have not placed their trust in God; or it may mean that God has a particular plan for a particular person, but a plan that in any case is encompassed by his love (1 Kings 17:9). This attitude may shock some people, and yet it is really the only reasonable, useful and honest attitude. Of course we know all the objections, and we expect the ridicule: "If it is true that God is concerned with these things, he's doing a pretty bad job of it." But these criticisms, like many of our teachings, turn man into an abstraction, in spite of human desires, sins, zeal for evil and destruction. The Bible teaches us, however, that God does not look at man in the abstract.

In the disorder of the Fall, whenever we defy God, we are given over to the consequences of our acts. This is not because of a commutative or an individualistic doctrine of justice. We are not talking about a given person who endures the consequences of such and such an act that he has committed. But in terrible solidarity, all must endure the acts of all. For the person who loves money more than other people is the cause of some people's poverty. Their misery is the mark of humanity's sin— everyone's sin. This is why it is hopeless to try to get rid of poverty by economic means. We can hope for no modification in the human condition unless we begin believing in God's love. This is the only possible way to break the dramatic chain of oppression and misery in which we live.

Second, we are called to *seek first* the kingdom of heaven and its righteousness; the rest will be given to us in addition. This implies a choice and a decision on our part. What have we decided to put in first place? This is the whole question. How will we occupy our life? If we truly put the search for the kingdom and for righteousness in first place, the problem of money becomes less pressing: it no longer looks like the central, decisive problem, and we no longer worry so much about it. When this happens, values are put in their proper place. Money is not first among them, however important it may be in providing for our material needs. This arrangement of the problem, in a hierarchy beginning with the kingdom of heaven, is essential if we are to be liberated from the power of money. But to accept this hierarchy, we must first agree to submit to God's judgment, for only when we submit to judgment will the kingdom of heaven take first place.

When a person thus *believes* in God's good intentions, and when a person *seeks* the kingdom, then money worries recede. This looks quite natural, but in truth it is the glorious work of God's victory in us.

Now this absence of worry does not in any way mean laziness or carelessness. We must not substitute human failings and sins for the freedom given by God. We are not called, like birds, to wait for our food to drop out of the skies. We are not birds, and we are called by God to exercise certain functions, to shoulder certain responsibilities. We must of course earn our living and fulfill our obligations to society, but as we do so, we know that these are not the most important things in our lives, and we ask God to calm our anxiety (for anxiety can coexist with work, and worry with money earned). We must be free with regard to money and the work which provides it. This attitude is truly a living testimony. It shows our trust in God better than any words could do.

Now in this question of trust, as in the preceding case, we must not hope to be able to hold on to both virtue and money, God and Mammon. There can be no synthesis or half measures. We are looking at a strict dilemma. On the one hand we may decide to receive our money from God. In this case, we recognize God's gift even when it is a paycheck, even when it results from something we have done. We receive this money from God. Because of this, we are quite sensitive about the means we will use to get this money: *these means must not dishonor God.* We have to judge what we do by the honor of this God who supplies our needs. If we do this, we are detached from money, we are free with respect to it, and we are at the same time free from worry.

Or, on the other hand, we may seek to receive this money elsewhere —whether we openly turn our back on God or whether, as is more often the case with Christians, we compromise ("I'm not hurting anybody," "God isn't concerned with these questions"). In this case, no matter how honest and scrupulous we are, we are getting our money from Satan. More than anything else, we want to make money. And we will manage to do so. We will probably even make more than if we had the first attitude. But we pay for it not only with our work but also with our freedom. This money is the cause of our worry, our slavery; it leads to death. No other choice is possible: there is no middle road, no third alternative.

Make Money Profane. The ultimate expression of this Christian attitude toward the power of money is what we will call *profanation.* To profane money, like all other powers, is to take away its sacred character. For although we usually think of profaning goods or values that are religious in a positive sense, it is just as possible to conduct such an assault against Satan and all he inspires. In this case, profanation is truly a duty of faith; it is part of the fight of faith spoken of in 1 Timothy (6:12), and it is no doubt what Paul means when he says Christ has "spoiled" the powers (Col 2:15 KJV).

This profanation, then, means uprooting the sacred character, destroying the element of power. We must bring money back to its simple role as a material instrument. When money is no more than an object, when it has lost its seductiveness, its supreme value, its superhuman splendor, then we can use it like any other of our belongings, like any machine. Of course, even if this relieves our fears, we must always be vigilant and very attentive because the power is never totally eliminated.

Now this profanation is first of all the result of a spiritual battle, but this must be translated into behavior. There is one act par excellence which profanes money by going directly against the law of money, an act for which money is not made. This act is *giving*.

Individuals as well as authorities know very well that giving attacks something sacred. They know full well that it is an act of profanation, of destruction of a value they worship. And this is why in all the world's legal systems in all ages, giving has been the most suspect act from a judicial viewpoint. Giving is surrounded with the maximum number of precautions. It is viewed with all possible suspicion. Of all acts, it is the most completely limited by law in its application and its effects. From the normal person's viewpoint, it is an abnormal act—almost unimaginable—and to give it a secure legal foundation, we are required to find reasons that are secret, inadmissible, immoral, and so forth. Indeed, if we managed to think of a pure and simple gift, this would be even more scandalous, for it would truly profane one of our gods.

In the biblical view, this is precisely how giving, which is a consecration to God, is seen. It is, as a matter of fact, the penetration of grace into the world of competition and selling. We have very clear indications that money, in the Christian life, is made *in order* to be given away. Note especially Paul's lovely text (2 Cor 8:10-15) based on the law about manna given in the wilderness: "He who gathered much had nothing over, and he who gathered little had no lack" (verse 15). If among fellow Christians we study Paul's law of equality, we see that money must be used to meet our needs, and that everything left over must be given away. There is no place for savings accounts. If it is necessary to earn money, it is "so that you may always have enough of everything and may provide in abundance for every good work" (2 Cor 9:8). If we really worked in order to give away the money we earned, that would undoubtedly set limits to the thirst for money which can possess us!

Now to whom should we give? Scripture says almost nothing about giving to the church, except for the tithe.[6] It speaks much more often about giving to God and to people. If we are going to rethink the problem of money in Christian life, perhaps we should not start by assuming it is an ecclesiastical problem.

Giving to God is the act of profanation par excellence. An object which belonged to a hostile power is torn from him in order to be turned over to the true God (Deut 26:1-11). This act obviously has only a spiritual meaning; it makes no sense at all from a social point of view. Socially concerned Protestants have, for the most part, entirely lost the meaning of this "free gift" to God, which is nevertheless a high expression of faith. The faithful Catholic has preserved its meaning much better than we have.

These gifts, given mostly during the Middle Ages to God's glory, are on the side of truth. Little matter that we can criticize some of their results such as the fact that the church profited from them, enriched itself and used them for capital—mistakes of church administration do not change the righteousness of a person's act of faith. We need to regain

---

[6]That is partly why we do not talk about money in church. But the main reason for this abstention can be found in H. Roux's excellent book, *L'argent dans l'Eglise* [Money in the church] (Delachaux and Niestlé). I have nothing to add to it!

an appreciation of gifts that are not utilitarian. We should meditate on the story in the Gospel of John where Mary wastes precious ointment on Jesus. The one who protests against this free gift is Judas. He would have preferred it to be used for good works, for the poor. He wanted such an enormous sum of money to be spent usefully. Giving to God introduces the useless into the world of efficiency, and this is an essential witness to faith in today's world (Jn 12:1-8).

But obviously giving to human beings also "desacralizes" money. We do not need to show the necessity of such giving, which is on the one hand an expression of charity (that is, of love) and on the other a spiritual act. It is the act by which man glorifies God and proclaims grace to other men. This is the special meaning of giving revealed in Isaiah 58:6-7. We see here that giving is truly an act of praise to God, almost an act of worship, replacing fasting. And in truth, the parallel between giving and fasting is not accidental. Both have to do with a privation that we accept as a sign of repentance, but also as a sign of grace and freedom.

We cannot measure the power of giving in human relations. Not only does it destroy the power of money, but even more, it introduces *the one who receives the gift* into the world of grace (remember the debtors in the parable of the unjust steward), and it begins a new chain of cause and effect which breaks the vicious circle of selling and corruption.

It is important that giving be truly free. It must never degenerate into charity, in the pejorative sense. Almsgiving is Mammon's perversion of giving. It affirms the superiority of the giver, who thus gains a point on the recipient, binds him, demands gratitude, humiliates him and reduces him to a lower state than he had before. Almsgiving acts this way because it is a money relationship and not a love relationship. And besides, it never includes the privation, comparable to fasting, of which Isaiah speaks. It never includes the gift of oneself. Quite the opposite, it affirms the self which is seeking its own righteousness and personal satisfaction. The Bible strongly reminds us of this by never distinguishing between those who are worthy of receiving gifts and those who are unworthy. The Bible speaks of the needy, those who lack the essentials of life. When we hear this appeal, we do not have to calculate if the poor person is needy by his own fault or by bad luck, if he merits our gift or not. These calculations belong to Mammon. They change giving into the restricted charity practiced by bad men of good will.

This gift of money can never be anonymous; it cannot be a duty which a person discharges. It is, on the contrary, an act that is closely linked with personal life. It is not the act of a person who is unacquainted with money, but rather of a person who knows how much he depends on money, how often money has been able to attack and possess him. This gift is made then in full consciousness of the power of money, not in ignorance of it. And that is why, ultimately, the gift of money presupposes and signifies the gift of oneself. This is clearly stated in the 2 Corinthians text where Paul, speaking of offerings and gifts, begins by saying, "For they gave . . . not as we expected, but first they gave themselves to the Lord and to us by the will of God" (8:3-5). Each gift that we give, then, ultimately expresses the consecration of our entire life. And because of this, only if our whole life belongs to Jesus Christ as Master can we truly desacralize money and give it away.

We should meditate on this fact and think of it each Sunday at the time of the offering. The offering is not a utilitarian act, and Protestants should stop thinking of it that way. (The church must be supported.) The offering, the moment of giving, should be for us the moment when we desacralize the world and show our consecration to the Lord.

But could we not ask if, as a result of our personal consecration, we should not give all of our goods? We think of the case of the rich young man to whom Jesus said, "Sell *all* that you have and distribute to the poor, . . . and come, follow me" (Lk 18:22). We absolutely must not try to sidestep this order, for example by separating the scriptural commandments given to perfected Christians from the others. We must, on the contrary, accept the order with all its vigor and its absolute character. Yet even so, this order is rather unusual; we do not find it frequently in either Old or New Testament. We must take it then as a possibility that is always present, a demand that we cannot avoid but that is given only in exceptional cases to people especially called to follow it.

This act will always result from a special vocation and is possible only to those who have this vocation. It is not a sine qua non of the Christian life, but each Christian is called to consider this vocation a possibility. At any moment of our life, this very demand may arise. At any moment we may be called to this vocation of giving all our money. If that happens we must not draw back because we are set in our ways, or even under the pretext that we have, by our good theology, found the proper balance and tension for a Christian in this difficult money situation. Above all, we must not allow this idea of vocation to keep us from hearing the call at all. In any event the call is never a constraint. And we do not have to make a sacrifice to God like pagan sacrifices or even like those of the Old Testament.

Remember that even giving all we possess will not pardon our sins or redeem us or draw God's attention to us. All this gift can do is express the enthusiasm of our love and gratitude, and because of this it is an act of freedom and joy. If we feel too much sadness in giving, if we feel torn or irritated, it is better not to give. But we must clearly understand what this means: it means that we are still under Mammon's power, that we love our money more than God, that we have not completely understood forgiveness and grace. This is what the end of the young man's story means. "He went away sorrowful" (Mt 19:22). He was sorrowful not so much because he had been given an order he could not follow, as because he felt far away from God's grace. And as long as this healthy sorrow lasts, if we are not right with God we will at least feel the call to give, which comes from God in his love. This act which only a few people carry out (and this does happen) must remain a call for all of us, a promise, but also a judgment on what we are not doing ourselves.

Thus if our giving is done in joy and in freedom, it can be total and complete, but it must not be total if we are going to be legalistic and turn it into a hardship. Consequently, total giving must never be the product of ecclesiastical rules or sociological fads. It is an individual act and cannot be the basis of behavior required of all Christians. Total giving is neither an economic system for handling money nor a danger to the stability of society. Total giving, always the exception, is a sign and a prophetic act.

It is a sign because it makes visible the grace of the invisible God. It is a witness of God's total gift to humankind.

It is a prophetic act because it announces the last days. This total consecration of money to God is an element of the kingdom of heaven in the midst of us, announcing the greater and final reality of God's kingdom. It is an element of the kingdom of heaven because it means that God's grace is worth giving up everything for—but this renunciation does not mean leaving things to go their own way; it does not in any sense mean that money is given back to Mammon. It is rather a surrender *into God's hands,* and thus it is a reintegration. For ultimately reintegration is what lies ahead for money, when the power of money admits its submission to Christ. This is one of the last-day promises announced in both Old and New Testaments.

Two matching texts, Haggai 2:7 and Revelation 21:24-26, show, as the old order disappears and the new is created, that money and riches will be given into the hands of the Lord. Everyone will crowd into the heavenly Jerusalem to bring what is most precious to them. It is *then* that God proclaims, "Money belongs to me." This affirmation is true only in the eschatological perspective. It is not unimportant to note that in Haggai, it is the "LORD of hosts" who says this, in other words, the "Lord, chief of the powers." This implies the disappearance or the total subjection of these powers, Mammon among them. Returning money to God is only one of many signs of this subjection of the rebel powers.

At the end of time, the power and the story of money will simultaneously be finished, and money will take its rightful place in creation. At the end of time we will be called to participate by giving everything. We herald this total gift, which will manifest God's glory on earth. Then and only then will we find once again the meaning of our life.

CHAPTER FOUR
CHILDREN
AND MONEY

U P TO NOW IT DOES NOT SEEM THAT MANY EDUCATORS HAVE studied this problem of money, although it is a highly sensitive area in the education of children. Very early, around age six if they go to school, children run up against money. Although they do not know what it is, they quickly understand its usefulness and force. They do not yet have any feeling of ownership about this abstraction, but they have already sensed its use, and through their parents they may have caught a glimpse of the importance that must be attached to it. All kinds of difficulties may arise out of interchanges with their playmates or because of their appropriation of someone else's money (not a theft, for they do not really understand that this could be owned by someone else). These difficulties can be one of our first ways of educating children in their relations with one of the powers of the world.

Realistic Teaching

If we continue taking Scripture as our guide, we will quickly notice that no express rules concerning the attitude of parents and children toward money are found there. Nevertheless we find firm guidelines in its revelation about the nature of money and in its general position of Christian realism.

A question like this one must remind us that in every situation, Christianity requires strict realism of us. This is not a philosophical opinion or a general doctrine of realism, but only a clear view of the real world which we must accept as it is. We must first oppose all idealism. In its popular form (refusal to see reality in favor of an ideal), with all the illusions and good feelings that it attaches to faith, such idealism turns God into "the good Lord" and Christmas into a children's holiday. It shows us the faith as we remember it from Sunday school and from songs our mothers sang. All this has nothing to do with Christianity. The Temple is not a refuge from the harsh world. But we must just as strongly reject philosophical idealism which would lead us to give priority to the world of ideas and values over the world of events and actions. Finally, Christianity objects to traditional spirituality with its package of religious values such as immortality and the preeminence of the soul over the body.

Confronted with all these distortions, God's revelation is remarkably realistic. It asks us to see the real world as it sheds light on it. Now the illumination that God's Word gives the world is particularly severe: our reality is a result of the Fall. Since that time the world has been radically estranged from God by its very nature. This reality is only a corruption, the kingdom of Satan, the creation of sin: in the natural world, we find nothing else. To say that in this world there is anything good, ideal or spiritual in itself is to deny revelation.

But this is not pessimism because revelation teaches us that God has not abandoned the real world. He continues to be present in it, he has undertaken an enormous work to transform it, and the kingdom of heaven is hidden in it. It is thus not pessimistic to affirm the existence of evil, for we know that God is the Lord; and because of our faith, we can have enough courage to look at the real world as it is. Because of our faith we can refuse to be deceived by the phrase we hear so often: "It's not so bad as all that." At the same time, to refuse to see this reality, to veil it with idealism or spirituality, is to betray God's Word and to rob God of his saving character.

This realistic position which fears neither words nor things must guide us in all educational work. We must never veil reality from children, idealize it or tint it with falsehood and illusion. But we must take into account each child's strength and reveal to each one only what he or she is able to bear, endure and understand about the real world. With a child, as with an adult, this ability comes only with an assured faith. As the child's faith grows, we can introduce the harsh realities of the world. Otherwise we would crush him under the weight of evil which he would not understand and against which he would have no hope. Such realism leads to a total education that is based on vigilance and evidence.

Foundations for Teaching. This realism assumes, first, that we will be looking at money as it is, or more precisely, as the Bible shows us it is in the world. We quickly learn that the reality revealed by the Bible is in every way what a scrupulous observation of the real world can teach us. This means that we must teach children what money is with its power and perversions. We must not let children live in a world of illusions. We must not give them all the money they want as if it were a natural and simple thing to do, but neither should we cut them off completely from the world of money. Too many Christian families, when dealing with their children, handle money problems only in the abstract. "No need to mix them up in such base and despicable things." But we forget that these children will then get their understanding of money from the world, which is not a better solution. Or if we succeed in completely cutting them off from money, once they are seventeen or eighteen years old they will be defenseless and without resources. Their innocence will be a trap for them; their purity will be an easy foothold for the demon.

We must then teach the child *progressively* both that money is necessary and that evil is attached to it. The need for money, all the work connected with it, the simple statement that we can't get along without it—these things children will understand quickly and will get used to easily. They will not, however, grasp the evil attached to money as easily. It will be very difficult to make them understand scriptural ideas that there is no good money or good use of money, that money brings evil in society and in human relations, and that it leads to evil in our personal and inner lives, with all the jealousy, hatred and murder that accompany the desire for money.

Undoubtedly all this can be taught, and many books or stories that the child will read take this approach. But this is not the best form of evidence. We should count much more on facts than on words to introduce the idea. Obviously the parents' example must be the foundation of this teaching, but above all we must take advantage of all circumstances—quarrels among children over money, social inequalities that children see themselves, thefts or strikes—all the events which, when explained, show the reality of the power of money along with the extreme danger that it entails.

Children must learn that people will sacrifice everything to have money; but like Spartan children before the drunken Helots, they are given this example to put them on guard so that they can protect themselves from a similar fate. In addition, children must gain experience by using money. Children will learn concretely, at their own level, what money is. I think it is vitally important that this experience be direct, that it involve real sums of money and real operations (simple purchases or sales) in proportion to each child's abilities.

The worst education about these ideas seems to me to be that given by games like Monopoly where children learn a complex financial management of abstract sums of money. In the real world children must know real things at their own level, for money is not a game and it quickly raises moral questions.

But such a method of teaching, especially concerning the evil provoked by money, risks falling into two dangers: moralism and negativism. Both are threats and both should be condemned. Moralism is a potential problem whenever children, having to choose between two attitudes, are almost automatically told by their parents which one is right. Once children have acquired certain habits, they will begin to act spontaneously as they have been taught. They will have been trained in a way that is not bad from a social standpoint but that in no way corresponds to life in Christ.

There is only one way to avoid moralism: by maintaining children's freedom and letting them choose their own behavior. As often as possible, children should make their own decisions on how they will handle money on the basis of what they have seen and heard. But they can be led to reflect on their actions afterward. Better that children make mistakes, act badly and reflect afterward than that they turn into robots who do good things that are not the fruit of their personality. This is a great problem for parents, who can only with great difficulty leave their children free to make mistakes.

The other danger is negativism. If children end up understanding (as they must) that money is bad (even when we do good things with it or use it well), they will tend to take a negative attitude toward it. Children tend to behave consistently; consequently, if something is evil, they keep away from it. They see things in black and white. Now this negative attitude is wrong from all standpoints. It is wrong because it leads to exactly the opposite of what is desirable: it leads to a false spirituality or a scorn for money. It is also wrong because negativism tends to spread and to affect other attitudes and judgments until it has become a way of life. When a child is negative on one point, we can easily see the contagion spreading into other areas of his personality.

The passive attitude in practical matters and the crushed spirit which result from negativism are serious failures in education. But in avoiding negativism we must not fall into the absurdity of "positivism," which is the usual tendency of today's education. This education is founded on the goodness of human nature, the validity of human thought and enterprises, and the justice of society. It shows vigorous and healthy optimism, but in God's eyes it is hypocrisy.

The only valid position is a dialectical one, but how difficult this is in education, for it assumes that children will give up their entrenched ideas and unilateral attitudes. Here are examples of what I mean by dialectical education in the area of money:

1. Children must know that money is not respectable, that we do not owe it honor or consideration, that the rich are not superior to others. At the same time, however, money is not contemptible. This is especially true of money their parents may give them, for it represents their work and is a way they have of showing them their love.

2. Children must know that money is necessary, but they must not draw the conclusion from this that it is good. Inversely, they must learn that it leads to much evil, but they must not draw the conclusion that it is useless. In other words, children must be taught to separate the ideas of *usefulness* and *goodness,* a separation that adults no longer make in our day.

3. When we teach children that money does evil, they will be led to see one side only. Either money does evil to those who have it by hardening their hearts, for example, or it does evil to those who passionately desire it by leading them to theft. Now it is essential to teach that money does evil both to those who have it and to those who do not, to one group as much as to the other. It is essential to teach that money does not leave us unscathed, whatever attitude we take or whatever situation we have been placed in by circumstances. In any case money first spoils our relations with people. Children must progressively learn to be wary of the effect money has on relations with adults and with friends.

In all this, the dominant idea is that Christian education must educate for risk and for danger. We must not shelter the young from the world's dangers, but arm them so they will be able to overcome them. We are talking about arming them not with a legalistic and moralistic breastplate, but with the strength of freedom. We are teaching them not to fight in their own strength, but to ask for the Holy Spirit and to rely on him. Parents then must be willing to allow their children to be placed in danger, knowing that there is no possible education in Christ without the presence of the real dangers of the world, for without danger, Christian education is only a worthless pretty picture which will not help at all when children first meet up with concrete life.

Possession and Deliverance

We must not live in a dream world. When young children use money, they cannot help being possessed by it. Such is its danger. Children will think it is marvelous to be able to buy so many lovely things; they will think it is fun, if they are from a rich family, to humiliate their playmates; they will be full of envy and bitterness if they are from a poor family. They will certainly admire the beautiful cars that money can provide, and perhaps will look down on their parents if they do not own one. There are so many signs of this possession, which can also be marked by many other feelings and impulses. However careful we may be in training our children, we cannot avoid this, at least not without breaking the child's spontaneity and falling into a legalistic moralism with all the repression it entails. For if what we have said about money is correct, there is no educational method, however subtle or refined, however psychologically astute or careful, adequate to check its power and to prevent possession. These are facts of a different order: the spiritual order.

Consequently the battle takes place on a different plane. Even though thorough educational work is necessary, it will not do a bit of good unless it is based on the real battle for the deliverance of children. If our educational method exposes children to the danger of possession, it must also protect them from it and deliver them by spiritual weapons, of which prayer is the first. It is not necessary to stress the importance of parents' prayers for their children. By this act the parents recognize that God is effectively in control of life and that only he can command money and free children from possession. This gives meaning to education which teaches right behavior toward money. This is neither magic nor method; it is the full liberty of God as expressed in grace responding to prayer. What we are going to say makes sense only if prayer is never neglected; prayer is the first act leading to deliverance.

This being the case, it is important to propose a type of behavior to children, perhaps as an example, but especially as a lifestyle. Undoubtedly money loses importance for children to the extent that their parents are themselves free from its power. Children who live in homes where the money question is the parents' central and obsessing preoccupation are inevitably conquered by this obsession. This is true whether the homes are rich or poor.

Children truly participate in the parents' deliverance that Jesus Christ offers. We cannot forget that biblically young children to about age twelve are part of their parents' lives. They not only depend on them materially, they also are spiritual and psychical parts of their parents. They are not yet their own persons, and consequently their parents' attitudes (whether internal or external) toward money are theirs. This explains why some parents who never talk about money in front of their children, or who try to behave in a dignified manner, but who in their inner lives are obsessed with money, have children who are also possessed by it. It is important that parents be free from possession inside as well as out. Otherwise children are possessed through their parents, even if their parents try to give them a just and healthy education.

And, to be sure, children seem to be excellent barometers of their parents' inner reality. They are not yet divided between their actions and thoughts: they are unities and directly express what they are. This is why instruction, examples or an atmosphere are far from enough. First of all parents must themselves have a right attitude toward money. Consequently when parents, by grace, are freed from this obsession, their children can hear and receive instruction, profit from education, acquire good behavior patterns.

But children's openness, their adherence to the truth lived out by their parents, is only temporary. Children are free with regard to money when their parents are free only until they become responsible for themselves. When this happens, the experiences they are called to undergo, the decisions they are called to make, will require them to face up to this power themselves, no longer through their parents. When this happens, what they become is no longer their parents' doing; it is their own business. But obviously if they have had their eyes opened to this struggle, they are better prepared and armed to endure it.

In short (and this is true whenever education is in the spiritual area), no educational method will work unless those who use it are themselves authentic, free from demon possession but able to discern it. All techniques are useless that fail to recognize this reality and try to accomplish by method alone what is really spiritual business. We cannot stint on this enterprise if we want to give our children something beyond a few more or less useful tricks for adapting themselves and getting out of scrapes. It goes without saying, moreover, that the prayer which accompanies this work makes no sense unless we are involved in the quest along with our children.

Seeking Things Above. The whole answer, however, is not found in general, indirect action (prayer and parental attitude). There is also specific and direct educational work to do. It makes use of all of today's pedagogical methods. But we must be aware of a major difference between Christian education and all other forms. When children are possessed by money, their resulting behavior will be sin: revolt against God and acceptance of the power of money. We are not speaking only of habits or of psychological illness, and consequently we cannot simply give free rein to the child's nature, leaving it to its natural goodness. We cannot simply arouse in each child the full development and expression of his personality, for this personality is evil. But we will not solve the problem of teaching behavior alone, behavior resulting from a moral code and expressing itself in virtues. If we are talking about sin, we must always remember Kierkegaard's observation that the opposite of sin is not virtue but faith. But how do we express this?

It seems that the most basic advice we can give is to "set your minds on things that are above" (Col 3:2). In all the details of their lives, children are called to offer their love to God in response to God's love and always to act from that starting point. If we do not always go back to God's love, we know how sterile our reasoning becomes. If we restrict ourselves to fighting money with moral or psychological methods, there comes a time when everything stops working, a time when we can find nothing more on which to base everything else. We must in real life rediscover the "things that are above" and derive moral and educational truths from them. The direct fight against money is ineffective without this. We must begin by giving a general direction to each child's life, leading each of them progressively to attachment to higher things, making the larger truths and realities penetrate their hearts. But this will necessarily be a slow work which will not immediately bear fruit. It is as children attach themselves to higher truths that they will pull away from lesser realities.

For there are two possible directions to take in this education about money. On the one hand we can try to stay on the level of the problem itself by considering money as a purely natural phenomenon, by looking at it from an economic and strictly human point of view. In this case we would need to use certain psychological tricks and, at best, an appeal to morality. On the other hand we can ourselves come to the point of mastering the questions money raises; we can see it in its profound reality. In this case we must lead children to the same understanding and judgment, because we are dealing with more complete truths and because we are living by these truths. We must be careful not to think there is anything mystical in this; we are simply saying that when a person truly loves something, there is little room for loving many other things.

If we love the "things that are above," we will be rather detached from the things that are below. We do not have to repudiate money or despise it: we have already seen that a major part of Christian education must be, by contrast, to teach the proper use and value of money. We have only to be sufficiently detached from it. Money loses its interest and its importance when we stop giving it importance and interest; we can do this only if we give importance and interest to something else. Otherwise our detachment will be only constraint and asceticism, and these are never advisable. We must not be a negative influence by depriving children of money or forcing them to do without. What is necessary is that children progressively detach themselves from money because another order of value attracts them.

Let there be no confusion: these values are not just any values. Humanism cannot produce this result even if it is very elevated. Neither intelligence nor virtue nor art will succeed in freeing children. We know how often in real life these things are subordinated to money. Not even Christian education of Sunday school or church membership are truly "the things from above"—only Jesus Christ himself and him alone. Children can learn that all contradictions are resolved in Christ and that the great power of money is only the power of a servant. And when children are joined to Jesus Christ, Christ's action is produced in them, giving them freedom and delivering them from passion.

We must be very careful. If children are thus detached from money, this is not at all a natural phenomenon, a simple psychological effect. It is not simply compensation where mechanically the moment children are interested in one thing they lose interest in other things. This does not have to do with their attention or habits. We must always remember what sort of thing possession by money is. We need the power of Jesus

Christ to dominate it, and it is Jesus' unforeseen, all-powerful and gracious act that causes this transformation of love in children as well as in adults. If we try to get by without this act which does not depend on us, our efforts will be in vain and our children will serve another lord.

A Generous Spirit. Of course problems of attitude and action arise, for it soon becomes necessary to make this detachment visible in action. Like everyone else, children must learn that Jesus' act of grace has consequences. One of the pillars of this education must be the parable of the unforgiving servant, the man who, with his own debt canceled, would not in turn cancel his friend's debt. If children realize what God's gift really is, each day and in each circumstance—if they understand that it is the gift of material things and even more the gift of Jesus Christ —they should spontaneously recognize in turn the meaning of giving. Children must be taught to give.

But they must not learn this by basing it on whatever natural generosity they may have, for this is exercised only to the extent that it costs nothing, and it often brings on reactions of selfishness or pride. To learn to give, children must choose the objects that they will give and the persons to whom they will give it. Gifts that are inspired, guided and directed by parents must be avoided. Let children realize little by little the necessity of giving, but leave the forms and applications of giving to their own free and independent choice.

This freedom, moreover, is an excellent way for parents to find out where they are in this education about money. Gifts should represent a true sacrifice on the part of children. Above all, parents must not give in to their children's spontaneous gestures by wanting to make up for what they have lost. Children will quickly learn that if they give something away, their parents will give them the same thing or something better in return, since they will be so happy and moved by the "lovely thing" they did. When this happens, giving becomes a calculation, and this is the worst education children could be given. It is essential that children learn to master themselves in order to do without what they have given away. Giving must be a serious test; let children know from this that their relations with other people as well as with God are also serious and important acts.

Another aspect of detachment from money has to do with the consideration children show for those around them. Superiority or inferiority complexes, with corresponding hatred for the rich or scorn and distrust for the poor, are easily created in children according to whether they are rich or poor. Sometimes the attitudes are reversed and the poor distrust the rich and take an attitude of superiority toward them, or the rich may have too high an opinion of the poor and may develop an inferiority complex. This is common nowadays.

However they are manifested, all these attitudes are totally bad because they all spoil human relations. One mark of freedom from money would be for children to pay no attention at all to how people are dressed or to their manners, to family connections or to wealth or poverty. Here begins the education which ends in Paul's affirmation: "I know how to be abased, and I know how to abound; . . . I have learned the secret of facing plenty and hunger, abundance and want" (Phil 4:12).

This is not as hard as we might imagine for children. Money becomes a barrier between people because of customs, mores and education. Children who are raised in a generous atmosphere, in an environment where people are not judged according to money, who are taught in a state school, will easily make contacts with children from different situations. The parents must only watch that their children not shock them and that they not begin to develop class consciousness. But make no mistake; this ability to be comfortable in all circumstances comes in reality only from the prior action of Jesus Christ.

It would be possible to give other examples of how to apply these principles, but real-life examples will appear as children develop and experience life, and these will be the wisest and most useful discoveries. And after all is said and done, after years of work, we will have only begun. For once children become adults they can throw over everything they have learned; they can want exactly the opposite of what was lived out in their families; they can choose to subordinate themselves to money in hopes that money will be given to them. All this is completely possible, for no Christian teaching method is an infallible recipe. Results are never obtained mathematically or guaranteed; they depend on the Holy Spirit for their effectiveness. Any teaching method that tries to get by without this is anti-Christian. We must then accept the fact that all our actions are subordinate to his, and that ultimately they will bear fruit only by the fertility of God's Spirit.

Learning to Live

But if this is the conclusion of a Christian education, and if we are left with such uncertainty, why attempt this training at all? This question introduces the study of two texts which seem to wrap up everything we have said. One is in the Old Testament, one in the New. Their differences (we could even say their contrasts) clearly set off the meaning of this education as well as the continuity of inspiration.

The first of these texts is in Proverbs (30:7-9): "Two things I ask of thee; deny them not to me before I die: Remove far from me falsehood and lying; give me neither poverty nor riches; feed me with the food that is needful for me, lest I be full, and deny thee, and say, 'Who is the LORD?' or lest I be poor, and steal, and profane the name of my God."

The second text, in the epistle to the Philippians (4:11-14), is in the context of Paul thanking the Philippian Christians for their gift of money: "Not that I complain of want; for I have learned, in whatever state I am, to be content. I know how to be abased, and I know how to abound; in any and all circumstances I have learned the secret of facing plenty and hunger, abundance and want. I can do all things in him who strengthens me. Yet it was kind of you to share my trouble."

Neither Poverty nor Riches. It is surely not arbitrary to put these two texts together. Both have to do with our situation when we want to obey God with respect to money, and both express this situation with the greatest accuracy. The Old Testament text is a prayer. This is remarkable in that Proverbs, which abounds in moral counsels, is very little oriented toward devotion or prayer. This underlines the importance of the fact that in this situation the author prays. This obviously implies a renunciation on his part: he cannot master this situation, he cannot control it; thus he prays to obtain from God what he cannot do for himself. Now what he cannot do, even with the aid of morality, is to create a right relationship with money. He sees the dangers perfectly clearly (and besides, he knows what money is) and realizes he cannot escape them.

If I become rich, I will deny my faith: the text says this as if it is an inevitable consequence, as if the writer, inspired by God, could not avoid falling into this temptation. Those who live in abundance do not know who the Lord is. They are satisfied with what they own and do not see what God would like to do in their lives. They need nothing and nobody. And this is the best way to exclude God. Modern advocates of universal economic prosperity know perfectly well what they are doing when they say that as a result of their system "religion" will disappear.

But poverty also seems insurmountable, and we have no way to rise above this situation either. Relationship with God is not more *natural* in poverty than in wealth; the poor are not better suited to it. Like the rich, they have a temptation which is difficult to overcome. They are tempted to steal. This is obvious.

But theft entails a hidden consequence, according to our text: it profanes God's name. Although the rabbinic translation uses the word *profane,* the Hebrew text literally says, "lest I take by force, lest I seize, the name of my God." And perhaps this is why this theft is so serious: it is not simply the theft of money or of bread but of God's name. The poor are indeed tempted to consider themselves righteous when they do evil. Because they are poor, it seems that evil is legitimate and that all God has to do is justify it; taking this a step further, the poor seize

God's name to make God responsible for the situation and consequently for the sin committed. Now in either case, wealth or poverty, human pride uses the situation in order to gain the upper hand and to set man against God.

Therefore in the presence of these dangers, "Solomon" asks not to be placed in these temptations. He asks that God give him only the "golden mean" in which he will be able to live according to God's will. This means that we should realize the importance of this intermediate situation. If we can obey God's will, it will first of all be because we are in the desired material conditions. Insofar as we cannot resist the take-over, the domination, of money in our lives, our only possibility is to avoid the problem objectively. We must avoid it by staying away from both of the two extremes, by avoiding the material causes of temptations. And this is perfectly wise.

But we must also avoid it *objectively* in the sense that we must expect a good result from objective conditions. If we are able to escape money's domination, it will be because the situation is objectively favorable. This means we must place ourselves in conditions that are objectively the best. To a great extent, this is the only possible attitude because, having measured money's power and the weakness of our faith, we know beforehand that we will succumb. But comfortable circumstances cannot be the result of good management; we are not master of our appetite or of the economy. We cannot establish exactly the favorable framework needed for our spiritual life. Left to ourselves, our will to power will carry us away.

Only God can establish good conditions. He gives bread. And all human wisdom in the Old Testament cannot go beyond this request for bare necessities with full trust in God and complete mistrust of man. It must be God who establishes the objective situation; it is a gift from him, which is why prayer is necessary. Those who are not delivered from their passion for money, who know that the enemy is unconquered, wait for God to make the situation the best possible to guard against aggression. By prayer and by the modesty of their requests these people show their dependence on God. They cannot do anything more than this.

Facing Plenty and Hunger. Now the text in Philippians is entirely different. Here we are looking at a man who says he is above objective, material conditions. Abundance and misery are identical situations through which he passes, and he goes through them by mastering them. Let us immediately set aside the human-centered argument which would attribute this to a difference in men. We have no reason to think St. Paul was stronger from a human standpoint than was the author of Proverbs. We have no reason to attribute to him a humanly superior spiritual life. And besides he himself did not think he owed his freedom to his virtues.

Neither is this the result of historical development. Without a doubt the visible power of money was much greater in the Roman era than in the year 600 B.C. If there is opposition between the two attitudes, it comes uniquely from the historical fact that Jesus Christ was born, died and rose again, which changes both the human condition and the authority of the powers. From then on our objective situation, whether economic or political, is not decisive for good or for ill. It does not necessarily bring about our collapse, nor is it enough to assure us a stable and well-organized spiritual life.

We are called by Jesus Christ to a life in which we no longer have to try to take out guarantees in order to be put in a situation where we can do God's will. Instead we should take risks. Of course in the Old Testament also there were situations where risks had to be taken for God, but these are not presented as the usual case. On the contrary, these were a priori impossibilities. Each time, a circumstantial miracle overcame the main obstacle in the material condition.

Today our situation is different. Whatever the objective circumstances may be, we are called to master them, and we can do it. We no longer have to hope for or fear a change in our spiritual life because of

economic or political conditions. Rather these conditions are pene-
trated, mastered and shaped by us if we truly have faith, that is, if we
take seriously the effective action of the Holy Spirit. What Paul is showing us here is really the victory of faith over money and everything
stemming from money, a victory that is possible only because money is
now a conquered power. This is not natural progress or a spiritualization of religion; yet money was an insurmountable power in "Solomon's" eyes, and now we see this power mastered, subjected, stripped
of its great seductiveness and authority, if not of its effectiveness.

Spiritually we can no longer fear money because on the cross Jesus
Christ took away its victory and its victims. From that time forward,
it has no longer been important to life in Christ whether one has money
or not. The only Christian attitude is contentment with whatever state
one is in. It is as pointless to make superhuman efforts to earn money
(or to develop the economy, productivity, and so forth, which amounts
to the same thing) as to feel guilty for having money (instead of feeling
guilty, all we need to do is put this money at the disposal of others,
exactly what Paul counsels). These are non-Christian attitudes which
Christians should leave behind.

Consequently the solution to the conflict we have with money is no
longer found in the objective situation about us, but in Jesus' victory
over the power of money, with whom we are associated. This is surely
what Paul is saying: "I can do *all things* in him who strengthens me."
Paul's own spiritual accomplishments, as we noted earlier, are not the
point. At the same time we recognize that Paul never minimizes the
importance of the question of money, precisely because he believes that
when we are able to live as well in abundance as in poverty, we can do
all things. Thus he presents this ability which comes from Jesus Christ's
victory as one of the most difficult of Christian virtues to obtain. When
we have overcome money, we can do *all things*.

But it goes without saying that to overcome money means to be able
to live the same way and be consecrated to God the same way whether

we have money or not. The response to the money question is thus not to flee from it; it is not to take the vow of poverty or asceticism, it is not necessarily to give up all one's possessions. All these actions would be looking for the answer in an objective remedy. But we must not deceive ourselves either—it is very difficult to be a true Christian in the midst of abundance. This can happen only if we are absolutely detached from our belongings. And we know how easily rich people can, hypocritically, declare that they are detached. If the rich apply Paul's phrase to themselves without manifesting, as Paul did, this detachment, they have reached the peak of possession by money.

Now when Paul reminds us of these things, he does so in a remarkable way. He does not pray that this will be the case; he observes a fact. It is not an attempt and a hope; it is simply true because Jesus' victory is an accomplished fact and because union with Christ by faith is another fact of human life. With respect to money we must not live in hope; we must make decisions and gain the victory over it immediately. We are not called to settle the problem of money at some future date in the kingdom of God, but right away.

Make decisions? This terminology is not customary, for a scrupulous theology which refers all power of willing and doing to God has made us unused to it. However, it is certainly what Paul implies when he says, "I *know* how to be abased," "I *have learned* to be content." This really involves an apprenticeship. And this is why these two texts make a fitting conclusion to a reflection on Christian education about money. When we are joined to Christ's victory, we must still draw out its implications: this is personal business. We each must learn. The fact that the Holy Spirit is victorious in us does not in any way make apprenticeship unnecessary. Although Paul is truly delivered from the power of money, he must still learn how to live in abundance and in poverty.

Here we must use a whole collection of human methods. It is not humanly easy to adapt to a condition of poverty; it is not humanly easy to know how to use money in a condition of wealth (for we have no right to waste it). These are not spiritual or psychological problems; they are concrete, practical problems, and this is where we have to undergo an apprenticeship. This is where understanding and reflection fit in. The apprenticeship begins then after the action of the Holy Spirit. And this is why we said that the education of children means nothing unless they are beneficiaries of the grace given to their parents. To the extent that they are not separated from their parents and that the parents live according to God's Word, education can be meaningful, valuable and necessary.

For this victory over money does not in any way get rid of material problems. When Paul speaks of his "trouble" ("affliction" in KJV), he uses a singularly strong word and shows that he is certainly not above these difficulties. He is suffering; he has suffered. The affliction of poverty is a terribly hard test, and the Holy Spirit's action does not transform us so that we do not suffer from it. Neither does it leave us indifferent to these things. Suffering remains suffering and a test. We are not made of iron, and we have not been turned into angels. Consequently in this new situation, the Old Testament text is not annulled. It is still in a sense an objective truth, like the valid prayer of one who is not yet assured of Christ's victory over the powers.

But are any of us easily assured of that? And do we have the right to take this assurance lightly? Nevertheless we are in a new situation. We are called to act by ourselves in all circumstances by the power given to us, which we must learn to use. Circumstances are no longer crushing or determinative. Material conditions and spiritual fatality have been conquered and subordinated. But if they are conquered in eternity, they must also be conquered on earth by human action, if we take Christ's victory and the power of the Spirit seriously. They will never be conquered by a general, collective, objective organization which gives each one what he is due; that, on the contrary, is the subordination of man to the power of money. They will be conquered by the individual free act, the act of each person who can do all things in Christ who strengthens him.

CHAPTER FIVE
THE HAVES
AND THE
HAVE-NOTS

A RAPID, *SUPERFICIAL READING OF THE BIBLE QUICKLY GIVES US* the impression of violent hostility against the rich. This is a consequence of the profound reality of money of which we have spoken, but it is all the more sobering to realize that living men and women are placed under this curse. For from one end of the Bible to the other rings out a curse on the rich. It is useless to try to get out of this by saying that it is talking about the wicked rich, or that this is the problem of another era. The prophetic and apostolic words are strikingly clear.

The Rich
It is not a particular action that is condemned; it is the very essence of the whole life of the rich, which is necessarily opposed to God. Apart from the exceptional cases we examined at the beginning—Abraham,

Job and Solomon—there is no righteous rich man, there is no good rich man. The three exceptions show us a spiritual attitude which makes Abraham, Job and Solomon something other than what the Bible calls "the rich," even though they all possess money. Judgment against the rich is always radical.

"Their houses are full of treachery; therefore they have become great and rich, they have grown fat and sleek. They know no bounds in deeds of wickedness; they judge not with justice the cause of the fatherless, to make it prosper, and they do not defend the rights of the needy. Shall I not punish them for these things? says the LORD" (Jer 5:27-29). And the prophet's description exactly matches the one given by the apostle: "Come now, you rich, . . . You have laid up treasure for the last days. Behold, the wages of the laborers who mowed your fields, which you kept back by fraud, cry out; and the cries of the harvesters have reached the ears of the Lord of hosts. You have lived on the earth in luxury and in pleasure; you have fattened your hearts in a day of slaughter. You have condemned, you have killed the righteous man; he does not resist you" (Jas 5:1-6).

It is unnecessary to recall the story of the rich man and Lazarus as reported by St. Luke. But in looking at these texts we could still have the impression that the problem concerns fraud and extortion. Now, we comfortably think, this is not the case with all rich people. Hard work and good business sense should not be placed in the same rank as these outrages. Indeed!

We will not get into the Marxist discussion of profit, which must exist whenever a worker is employed; we will not say that the passage in James ratifies this attitude toward profit, and that it is impossible to act any other way, however honest the rich person may be; this would lead us too far afield. But it is sufficient to think of the text in Ezekiel on the wisdom of the rich to be warned about such distinctions. The Word of God is addressed to the prince of Tyre: "You are indeed wiser than Daniel; no secret is hidden from you; by your wisdom and your understanding you have gotten wealth for yourself, and have gathered gold and silver into your treasuries; by your great wisdom in trade you have increased your wealth, and your heart has become proud in your wealth" (Ezek 28:3-5). Here we are looking at the acquisition of wealth by a proper conduct of business—and still the result is the same. This accumulation of money is always linked with sin, whether at the beginning or as a consequence.

Even more characteristic is this phrase in Ezekiel: "In the abundance of your trade you were filled with violence, and you sinned" (Ezek 28:16). Evil was not present at the beginning of his activity; it was the abundance of his trade that provoked it. Thus it is the extreme development of this quest, this desire, this accumulation of money that necessarily generates sin. Note incidentally that this is addressed to Tyre: thus condemnation of the rich is not reserved for Israel's rich alone (or in our time for rich Christians, who seem guiltier than the others). It is for everyone.

Now in the presence of these observations about the conduct and life of the rich, Scripture lays down God's curse: "*Woe* to him who builds his house by unrighteousness, and his upper rooms by injustice; who makes his neighbor serve him for nothing, and does not give him his wages; who says, 'I will build myself a great house with spacious upper rooms,' and cuts out windows for it, paneling it with cedar, and painting it with vermilion. Do you think you are a king because you compete in cedar?" (Jer 22:13-15). This prophecy addressed to the king is ultimately valid for all rich people. It clearly shows confusion between the true power which comes from God and the power of riches. This confusion brings a curse with it. Isaiah says the same thing: "Woe to those who join house to house, who add field to field, until there is no more room, and you are made to dwell alone in the midst of the land. . . . [Woe to those] who acquit the guilty for a bribe, and deprive the innocent of his right!" (Is 5:8, 23). And how could we pass by the word that summarizes all the rest without exception, Jesus' severe statement of the curse: "Woe to you that are rich, for you have received your consolation" (Lk 6:24).

This curse is first expressed in the texts by certain material events. Ezekiel announces as the conclusion of his prophecy: "Therefore, behold, I will bring strangers upon you, the most terrible of the nations; and they shall draw their swords against the beauty of your wisdom and defile your splendor" (Ezek 28:7). And similarly, "Surely many houses shall be desolate, large and beautiful houses, without inhabitant" (Is 5:9).

But this only announces the greatest wrath, the greatest curse that comes upon the rich at the end of time: "Therefore, as the tongue of fire devours the stubble, and as dry grass sinks down in the flame, so their root will be as rottenness, and their blossom go up like dust" (Is 5:24). And James picks up the same theme: "Come now, you rich, weep and howl for the miseries that are coming upon you. Your riches have rotted and your garments are moth-eaten. Your gold and silver have rusted, and their rust will be evidence against you and will eat your flesh like fire" (Jas 5:1-3). We are thus in the presence of a final, eternal condemnation, whose means is the same in all the texts—fire. It is not necessary to try to find an analogy between the rich man's annihilation by fire and his devouring passion for money, but we must nevertheless emphasize that this power of fire is more often mentioned for the rich than for anyone else.

To this we add an unusual feature of James's pericope: it is the rust of the gold and the silver which is working. The person tied to money is devoured by the money itself. A terrible justice gives the rich over to what they wanted to possess. Wanting money above all else, they will be joined forever to it. They will be possessed by it, turned over defenseless to it, so that its fate will be their own—rusty money, doomed to destruction. This rust witnesses against the rich. It attests that they are joined to that which is perishable, and like a fire it devours their flesh.

Jesus Christ tells why the rich are thus condemned: "Woe to you that are rich, for you have received your consolation" (Lk 6:24). This is not quite as simplistic as anti-Christians would have it: "God punishes people for being happy on earth." No, but the rich have no need for God's aid or consolation or love. The power of their money is enough help for them, and the comfort of their money gives them all the hope they want. They do not need the Comforter, that is, the Holy Spirit, who is also their advocate before God.

The attitude and situation of the rich are the exact antithesis of love as we discussed it in chapter three. Now, if the rich do not need God's love on earth, they will not find it in heaven either. This is a simple continuity. It is logical and regular, we could even say normal. But to be deprived of God's consolation and love while standing in his presence is itself the devouring fire. It is to be delivered, with no further appeal, to the destruction of money.

On earth, when people offer themselves to money, there is always the possibility that they will change their course and open themselves to God. Nothing is yet final. But with death, the situation that people want becomes definitive. This is how it is a devouring fire: people stay eternally, with no possibility of change, with the comforter they have chosen. They are thus outside the kingdom of God. "It is easier for a camel to go through the eye of a needle than for a rich man to enter the kingdom of God" (Mt 19:24).

And looking at this severe punishment, we understand the disciples' fearful question: "Who then can be saved?" (verse 25).

The Poor

Without money, people are only paupers. They stand outside society and have hardly any place or function. We can almost say with Marx that in our world people exist only because of what they have, and when they have nothing, they do not exist. This is true in all societies, not only in capitalism, but the superiority given to material things in capitalism or socialism (it all comes to the same thing) makes this phenomenon more obvious and more severe in our time.

The Bible did not have to wait for either the capitalist constitution or Marx's teachings to give us the most complete and powerful teaching regarding the poor that has ever existed.

This light is horribly troublesome, and periodically the church tries to obscure it. It is helped in this work by all the forces of the world. In truth, this light shines pitilessly on the whole man as well as on one of the most solid bonds in the world, the bond of money.

The power of money is not completely disgraced until we have seen what and who the poor are.

Poor in Money and Spirit. The first major observation that these texts permit us to make is that our habitual distinctions between certain categories of poor persons are invalid. There are not poor who are ashamed to beg versus resentful poor, virtuous poor versus vicious poor, poor in money versus poor in spirit.[1] We absolutely cannot distinguish between them, even though the idea of poverty joins the whole group together. Poverty must simultaneously involve money and spirit. The Hebrew term meaning "poor person" indeed implies both poor in money and poor in spirit: the person who is humble. This term implies at the same time a gentle, kind-hearted moral attitude and, in another area, misery inflicted from outside: oppression, outrage. The two ideas of humiliation and humility intermingle.

---

[1]The Hebrew word *poor* is translated by the following four terms:

1. *ʿānāw* or *ʿānî* means, as we indicate in the text, "unfortunate," with the double meaning of poor in money or poor in spirit. It is also the one who is humble, meek, humiliated. This term is related to the verb *ʿānāh* (the root of our substantive adjective), implying the idea of humiliation and prostration. But we must also emphasize here that this verb, in its most general sense, means "to respond." It is thus not a chance deduction when we join the idea of responsibility to the presence of the poor. The poor person is indeed a person who requires a response; his very existence questions our lives. This is assumed by the relation of meaning that we will emphasize later.

2. *ʾebion* has a meaning that is more marked by the idea of indigence. The economic character of poverty is more stressed here. In this sense, the Ebion is a man who is wanting. But the spiritual meaning is certainly not absent. We need only remember the religious nature of the Ebionites in Israel; on this all historians seem to agree. But we can also wonder if the root (*ʾbh*) which includes a tendency to consent, to acquiescence, does not already assume that the Ebion has a certain attitude toward his material poverty. It may mean more than his humiliation before God.

In any case, as A. Causse, whose work on the Ebionites is foundational, points out:

The first element of this poverty, then, is economic: "If you lend money to any of my people with you who is poor, you shall not be to him as a creditor" (Ex 22:25). There is no real poverty that is not material. We affirm that the Bible habitually rejects the possibility of poverty in spirit when a person is rich in money. It is much too easy when we are rich in money to talk as if we were poor, to speak of spiritual detachment, and so forth. The Bible expressly condemns this attitude. We do not need to tell the story of the rich young man, which is characteristic enough; but it is good that we encounter a text in Proverbs which is singularly explicit about this: "[A man] pretends to be poor, yet has great wealth" (Prov 13:7). It is worth noting that the Hebrew word used here is not the one designating the authentic poor person, but rather a pejorative term whose root implies the idea of sin, impiety and lying.

But the second element of this poverty is spiritual. It is not enough to be poor in money. It is also important to be poor in spirit. The inner attitude of humility is necessary. This is neither kindness nor virtue; it is simply an agreement between spiritual life and material condition. The poor who do not take poverty on themselves are described the same way as the rich who play at being poor: "A poor man does not hear rebuke" (Prov 13:8, margin). "Poverty and disgrace come to him who ignores instruction" (Prov 13:18). "[Do not] give me . . . poverty, . . . lest I be poor, and steal, and profane the name of my God" (Prov 30:8-9).

"The praying person calls himself either 'the humble one' or 'the poor one': 'ani or 'ebion . . .'"

3. *dal* implies the idea of scantiness, weakness, social inferiority. This term is most interestingly used to indicate belonging to the poor class, the lower class.

4. The fourth term is not comparable at all: *rāš* is most often used in the Proverbs. It also means poor and is connected with a root implying the idea of need, but if from a material standpoint it means poverty in money, it does not have the same spiritual meaning at all. Rather, it is one of a whole group of terms implying the idea of sin or of poison. It has a negative meaning from a spiritual standpoint.

This difference does not mean that there are good and bad poor people, but that material poverty alone, unaccompanied by spiritual poverty, is a negative state without special significance.

In other words, poverty is no justification for sin. Sin is sin, even if it is committed by a poor person. In light of this, it is twice recommended not to judge unjustly *in favor of* the poor (Ex 23:3; Lev 19:15). The poor have a right to justice and not to injustice in their favor.

What we learn from the different Hebrew words used to designate the poor is that the poor are no longer objects of God's favor when they commit injustice, revolt, sacrilege and lying. They then lose their right to be considered among the righteous poor, and even if they have no money they take their place among the rich.

This double element of poverty is underlined by the oft-explained way the beatitudes are written. On the one hand Matthew says, "Blessed are the poor in spirit," "Blessed are those who hunger and thirst for righteousness." On the other hand Luke says, "Blessed are you poor," "Blessed are you that hunger now."

This difference is not based primarily on the writers' opposing concerns (one more spiritual, the other more social, with "Ebionite" tendencies), nor on the effect of time (Luke wrote first, with an intervening movement of spiritualization in the church). These facts may be correct, but they do not exhaust the meaning of the parallelism. This difference expresses precisely the double characteristic that Israel recognized in the poor. In this double characteristic, nothing must be omitted because as soon as one of the elements is left out, the idea of poverty itself disappears.

Besides, this idea implies a third element, contained in the root of the word: oppression and persecution. We will look again later at this condition of the poor.

But the poor are also depicted as those who bring together in themselves all possible miseries: they are sick, abandoned, misunderstood, sold and betrayed. This poverty looks even more like the visible mark of sin. For we must not forget that for Jewish society even at this time, wealth is a sign of blessing. The poor are cursed by God. And we cannot silence the wrath of Job, who refuses to understand how he, the righteous one, has become poor—how he has lost his fortune, his health and his family while deserving only God's blessing for his good conduct. We are always tempted by this interpretation: "If he is poor, it's because he deserves it!" Thus we interpret poverty as a sort of divine retribution for sin, and this human judgment, which sometimes becomes the judgment of the poor on themselves, closes the door of hope to them. They can no longer hope that their condition will change, for they feel that the whole world is against them; they condemn themselves, and the conviction of God's judgment weighs heavily on them.

They have no more worldly resources on which they can depend. They are totally destitute, in fact and in mind, in means and in spirit; it is this double destitution that makes them poor. But as soon as one of these privations disappears, they are no longer the poor spoken of in Scripture. The poor person in the Bible lives in the world as God's question to everyone. "How can this person live? How is it possible? Who am I before this person?

No Hope but God. The poor in the Bible are also the just, the righteous. They are like children. Jesus gives us a child as an example ("unless you turn and become like children"—Mt 18:3) because children are weak. They need someone else and they know it. The poor are the just not because they are virtuous and good, nor because they carry the future and history with them, nor simply because they are poor, but because they can have no hope other than God himself. Everything has been taken from them, apparently even God, yet against all reason it is to God that the poor raise their cry. It is moreover not essential (and Scripture stresses this) that they do this consciously. The poor do not need to be theologians. To whomever their cry for help is raised, so long as it is not to the worldly powers, it is raised to God (Jas 5:4) like the cry of the earth was addressed to God after Abel's murder. The poor truly wait for their help and freedom and righteousness from God.

When this is not the case, when the poor expect help to come from another source such as majority rule, revolution or the government, then they enter the ranks of the rich, however physically miserable they may be. But this never entirely ceases to be the case because humility, this waiting for God alone, is part of their name. And that is where their righteousness is found.

They are righteous *because* God responds to their cry from the bottom of the pit. Justification—not a game, but God's response to authentic despair—is given to them. God is on the side of the poor. It is appalling that the church has been able to forget this. "As for me, I am poor and needy," says the psalmist, "but the LORD takes thought for me. Thou art my help and my deliverer; do not tarry, O my God!" (Ps 40:17). "For the LORD hears the needy" (Ps 69:33). "For he stands at the right hand of the needy, to save him from those who condemn him to death" (Ps 109:31). And as a vision of the end: "The meek shall obtain fresh joy in the LORD, and the poor among men shall exult in the Holy One of Israel. For . . . all who watch to do evil shall be cut off" (Is 29:19-20). God gives them justice; they are just. This helps us understand what we were saying earlier: the poor cannot resort to injustice for help; injustice must not be done even in their favor.

Now we know that God's justice is expressed in the supreme example of his love: the gospel is made for the poor. The rich can see nothing in it, can understand nothing, cannot know its depth and truth. "The *poor* have good news preached to them" (Mt 11:5). What need would the others have, whether their wealth is in money or in spirit, of good news? Jesus, to affirm the identity of the Old Testament with this good news, goes back to the central assurance that God's act is to draw near to the poor. In Luke 4:18 he cites Isaiah 61: "The Spirit of the Lord is upon me, because he has anointed me to preach good news to the poor. He has sent me to proclaim release to the captives and recovering of sight to the blind, to set at liberty those who are oppressed."

Thus Jesus affirms that he himself is God's response to the call of the poor. He is God's response because he is himself the Poor One. In him is realized all that the old covenant said about the poor. He is the one who, being rich with all God's wealth, divested himself of it to become totally poor, to the point of being abandoned by his Father (Phil 2:4-8; 2 Cor 8:9). He is poor, in the material sense, for he lives off the charity of others. He is a wanderer; he has no house, no peace and quiet, no material security.

Yahweh's Poor One. He is poor in the spiritual sense, for he has nothing on his own. He is God's dependent. And as such, adopted by God, he becomes "Yahweh's Poor One." He lives only by the Spirit which God gives him. He submits to the risk that comes with God's gift; he retains nothing to affirm or assert himself, even spiritually. He is the Poor One in oppression because he is the Righteous One who has been unjustly condemned and because in him, as nowhere else, humility and humiliation are brought together.

Now what is asked of every person is to "walk humbly with your God" (Mic 6:8). Thus, in truth, the Old Testament texts about the poor are prophetic of Jesus Christ. Of course this idea of the poor and the spiritual meaning we have seen in them are developed in a given historical framework and are no absolute. It is primarily after the exile, under the prompting of Jeremiah and then of Ezekiel, that we first see this idea that the poor man is the true servant of Yahweh. He is not only wretched; he is also the Spirit's beggar and God's dependent.

Half a century before the deportation, however, Zephaniah was already proclaiming that only the poor please God, and that they alone had a chance to be saved in the coming judgment (Zeph 2:3). Zephaniah also announces the establishment, after this judgment, of a humble and poor people who will look to Yahweh's name for their salvation (3:12-13).

This is evidence then of some understanding of this concept of the poor, well before its meaning was generally accepted, before a national event could justify its elaboration.

But there is no doubt that the meaning of poverty was revealed to the eyes of the chosen people throughout the sixth century. It is possible that the link between poor and pious was made because adherents to Yahwism were recruited from the poorer classes. This is only a guess. In any case this has never led, as Van der Ploeg showed, to making poverty a religious ideal in the Old Testament setting.[2] But little by little the idea that the poor are righteous led to making poverty a necessary condition of piety. If we restrict our investigation to historical events, we see only Israel's distortion of the truth about the poor.

The dramatic recognition of the poor effected by Jeremiah—a man who suffered, was persecuted, was isolated, who had no strength but God's and to whom God promised nothing but more suffering—has nothing to do with piety. Neither does relinquishment based on fear of judgment, as in Zephaniah.

The authentic Poor One who is revealed to us is not the Pious One, but the Righteous One. But what do we expect man to do with this, if not reduce God's grace to his own size? This is what happens in Israel. The exilic revelation is transformed into religious business. The word *'ebion* becomes a technical expression in religious language to mean "the pious one."

A distortion follows, comparable to the Puritan distortion we already denounced, that wealth is a proof of blessing. The poor appropriate God's grace for themselves and change God's righteousness into piety. Thus in the second century before Jesus Christ, sects of poor people, proud of their own righteousness, fiercely nationalistic and pietistic, develop. But the numerous surviving texts of their literature show us that they are at an infinite distance from the poor who are beloved by God.

According to Gelin's pertinent observation, we must remember that in the parable of the publican and the Pharisee, it is the publican who is rich in money and the Pharisee who is poor in money, for poverty

---

[2]Ploeg, "Les pauvres d'Israël," *Etudes sur l'Ancien Testament* 7, 1950.

is one of the conditions of the piety he observes.[3] But as soon as this poverty becomes a factor in human self-justification, it loses all its value. The poor Pharisee is a hypocrite.

If we stick with the historical explanation of this relation between poverty and righteousness, it leads us to a current that takes us quite far from Jesus Christ. For we must not take away from our texts their *other* dimension—their prophetic dimension. When Jeremiah speaks as he does, it is as a prophet that he is speaking and living. Already he sees Jesus Christ in the condition of the poor. He alone will be the Poor One in his fullness. When on the cross he adopts the twenty-second Psalm ("Why hast thou forsaken me?"), he addresses to God the very word of the poor.

The Old Testament texts, more than anything else, prophesy of this Incarnation, but they are also concerned with people. For every prophetic text also sheds light on humanity through Jesus Christ. And if the Poor One is Jesus Christ, if the Old Testament gives the poor this dramatic and immense importance because of Christ's assumption of their condition, this also means that all poor people are imperfect images of this perfect fulfillment.

Images of the Poor One. Like the texts, poor persons themselves point to the Poor One. The meaning, the dignity and the truth of the Poor One reflect on the poor who are thus clothed and authenticated. It is not because of their virtue or even their condition that they are God's question to the world. It is simply because they are the permanent, constant reflection of Jesus Christ himself. Thus we understand why it is justice and righteousness they are waiting for; for it is justification in Christ that is given to them. We also understand why Jesus Christ utters these words which often leave us troubled and upset: "You always have the poor with you, but you will not always have me" (Mt 26:11). It is true that the Poor One does not stay on earth, but he leaves his

[3]Gelin, *Cahiers Sioniens,* 1951.

representatives, his reflection. The poor must be present among us to the end of the world in order to disturb our pride and our consciences by continually asking God's question of our lives.

Jesus sometimes pushes this relationship between the poor and the righteous to the point of identification. He does this in the parable of the judgment, where he says: "As you did it to one of the least of these my brethren, you did it to me" (Mt 25:40). Here we see, in each poor person, the person of Jesus Christ himself. And we finally understand how and why the church is essentially a gathering of poor people. "Not many of you were wise according to worldly standards, not many were powerful, not many were of noble birth," says Paul to the Corinthians (1 Cor 1:26). He presents this as an accepted fact, but also as a just and good reality, as the way things ought to be.

The church cannot be an assembly of the rich; it is made for poor outsiders. Jesus Christ came to call those who are sick. "Those who are well have no need of a physician," he said, "but those who are sick" (Mk 2:17). And he came to call the poor *outsiders*. In the parable of the feast, all these wretched ones were invited. The body of Christ, the body of the Poor One, can be composed only of the poor, not because they are superior, but simply because in their situation they are in accord with the person of Jesus Christ.

This should be a constant sorrow to the members of our churches who are aware of it. For our churches are not like that. And this is why, as we shall see later, our congregations can never completely be the body of Christ.

In any case this gospel affirmation allows us to object to any tactic whose intention is to Christianize the powerful: millionaires, cabinet members, generals, company presidents. It is true that if we want to have political and social influence, we will have to start there. But we must ask these powerful people the question raised by the poor. Either they will stay powerful and the church will cease being a true church and their social influence will amount to nothing, or they will accept the question asked by the Poor One and they will cease being powerful.

This certainly does not mean that we should not evangelize the powerful! But we must realize, when we do, that conversion will put the powerful person into the greatest imaginable quandary. Above all, evangelism must not have the intention of conquering a social or political force. This is another way of betraying Jesus Christ.

Finally we must add a warning. We must not let material poverty take precedence; we must not simplify all this by saying, for example, that the poor (from an economic standpoint) are themselves the righteous. All we are saying is that every poor person can be righteous. Even less should we make hasty generalizations and say, for instance, that the proletariat, in the Marxist sense, are the poor in the biblical sense, or that the working class by nature represents the poor, or that the working-class party is the party of the poor. This, unfortunately, is a tragic lie, for the Communist party is a typical example of the rich and powerful as described in Scripture. It is the party that uses the poor, quite a different thing from being the party of the poor. It is the party which raises their hopes, no doubt, but which takes them away from the place the Bible says they should go, away from God. And precisely because the party clothes the hopes of the poor with power, dictatorship and hatred, it transforms the poor into what Scripture calls *rich*. It is the real murderer of the poor. And if someone reminds us that the Communist party alone has not disappointed the hopes of the poor, whereas the church has betrayed them (and this is true), we must remember that Satan, in the Garden of Eden, had not yet betrayed Adam and Eve's hopes either.

I am not unaware of Communism's good points; I am simply warning that when the Bible speaks of the poor, we cannot identify this with the most powerful party in the world.

God's Question and Our Response

The Bible firmly plants the poor in the very center of truth and life. Each of us must face up to the poor.

The Poor One and poor people in general are God's question to us. God gives us responsibility in the world by asking us a question which we have to answer. This question is constant, permanent, living, for "you always have the poor with you." We cannot sidestep this question, for we are always in contact with the poor, and each one of them puts God's big question in human flesh.

This question is addressed to everyone. We do not have to understand theological explanations, we do not even have to be Christian, to hear it. It is part of the silent interrogation that God is always carrying on and behind which he hides himself. And people can respond without knowing to whom, ultimately, they are responding. This is what Jesus reports in the parable of the Judgment.

"When did we do this for you?" ask the elect. And inversely the damned ask, "But when did we refuse to do this for you?" And Jesus answers, "Truly, I say to you, as you did it to one of the least of these my brethren, you did it to me" (Mt 25:40).

Both those who gave and those who refused to give were ignorant of any teaching about the poor. Nevertheless they faced this question about their lives, and they had to respond. For, whether we like it or not, we have to answer either positively or negatively. Our whole attitude is a response. Scripture reveals that our attitude toward the poor is our response to God's question. We all can find our place and get involved with this question, which appears to concern economics or human feelings; but behind this question, a spiritual decision is ultimately demanded of us.

God adopts the poor in order to put us all in question, and it is certainly our all that is put in question if we understand the place and power of money in every person's life. Now with regard to God's poor, we are all on the same side—all, with the Communist party, on the side of the rich according to the Bible.

The Bible calls anyone who has no real need of God's help *rich*. This means that it is not enough to imagine that we need his help, or even to desire it. The person who, humanly speaking, has everything, who has human power, does not need the Lord. For his desire for the Lord is only for a supplement, a buttress, to his security. The false wisdom of the rich says, "God helps those who help themselves." And Scripture answers, "Only believe." When we know how to solve our problems ourselves, we have no need of the Lord's help except as a tradition or to assuage our doubts ("just in case . . ."). The Lord does not respond to this.

We have a choice to make, the choice which God constantly places before the people of Israel: either an alliance with Egypt, the Assyrians, and so forth, or an alliance with the Lord. There is no way to have both. It is God or Mammon. And if we want Mammon, that means that we do not really need God. The rich are faced with this agonizing choice. In our world, we solve our problems all alone with our technology, our science, our money, our political parties; God does not answer because we do not call him. The poor do not call on him, and those who call him are the rich.

The Church Is Rich. We in the church are among the rich. Not only because the church is largely middle class (I will not take up this oft-discussed theme, but it is true that by occupation, social rank, culture and money, Christians are usually rich), our Christianity itself contributes to this. It is almost impossible for us to be poor in spirit. We have the church, worship, prayer and the Bible. We have received the wealth of God's revelation. Jesus Christ "became poor, so that by his poverty you might become rich," says Paul (2 Cor 8:9).

This is not the problem of Pharisaism, or rather it is only one aspect of it. It is not the attitude that glorifies the church and condemns the sinners outside it, but in the best of cases it is the almost inevitable attitude that we own God's revelation. The church becomes the proprietor of God's riches, even when Christians have much humility, piety and fidelity. Compared with the poor who have only the sense of being abandoned by God, who have no social structures or morality to guide them, no Word of God to make their way clear, we are truly the spiritually rich.

But in the church, only Jesus Christ is truly the Poor One, and those who pretend to be publicans are really poverty-stricken Pharisees. This condition, in which we find ourselves and which we cannot escape (for how could we be humble about the grace which is given to us!), explains why the church can never be entirely, truly, the body of Christ. For the true church, which is the assembly of the poor, immediately makes these poor people rich in spirit.

The rich are confronting the poor. The rich are asked the question that God asks the whole world, and the rich are responsible—called to respond—before God to the question of the poor, which is God's question. They are called to answer for the world in the world's name. But this is not easy, and it is a heavy charge that God gives them.

Scripture shows us that the rich do not like this question at all, and this is why they do not like the poor at all. Scripture describes the usual attitude of the rich: "The poor use entreaties, but the rich answer roughly" (Prov 18:23). This is not an exception; it is a general observation, a veritable sociological law, like almost everything else found in Proverbs. "The rich rules over the poor" (Prov 22:7). The rich cannot do otherwise; they are inhabited by a spirit of power and of domination. They oppress the poor. "The poor man and the oppressor meet together; the LORD gives light to the eyes of both" (Prov 29:13). And the rich build all their wealth on the poverty of the poor; they are rich and they deprive the poor of their wages (Jas 2:2-6).

In addition, the rich look down on the poor and crush them not only economically and materially but also spiritually. They do this with contempt ("The poor man's wisdom is despised, and his words are not heeded"—Eccles 9:16), with neglect and even with hatred ("The poor is disliked even by his neighbor"—Prov 14:20). If there is one thing we cannot tolerate, it is this question, and the one who raises it becomes an object of hatred. "All a poor man's brothers hate him" (Prov 19:7). It does not seem necessary to go further and add to our collection the much better-known texts in the Psalms. There we see the psalmist's constant lament for the poor because they are oppressed, detested and mocked, because people try to trap them and strip them of what little they have.

In real life the rich crush the poor by the system (whether a capitalist system built on exploitation or a communist system built on oppression) or by a personal attitude. Which way does not make much difference; the same reality is present. Ultimately the rich seek to kill the poor. The attitude behind this is that of Cain killing Abel or the Pharisees killing Jesus. This happens because the rich are exasperated by constantly being called into question by God through the poor.

Avoiding the Question. The rich do not accept God's question, for, as we will see, this question is not easy. It is not safe to accept responsibility, and it requires much courage to confront this situation. Thus the rich try to get rid of the question. They try to turn away from it, like Adam running away from God's question after the Fall. They try to break the sharp point of the sword of the Lord which is piercing their flesh, this intolerable insistence seen in the eyes of the poor. So they kill the poor.

This is the real reason for the amazing problem that in all societies, the rich have detested the poor. Why, when precisely the rich are the powerful, the superior, the strong, do they set themselves against the poor? Why the persecution of the Jews, the massacre of slaves, the hatred of the proletariat? We can find of course all the psychological and sociological reasons we could want. But none of these reasons is definitive; none really explains. They all depend on our hatred for God, our rejection of God's questions, our refusal to accept responsibility. They all relate to the fact that the poor are a temporal reflection of the Son of God, the Poor One.

By acting this way, the rich condemn themselves. And this happens even if they have not gone as far as murder: we need only think of the story of the rich man (we are not told that he was a bad rich man, simply rich) and Lazarus (Lk 16:19-31). The rich man did not hurt Lazarus. But in this encounter he never wanted to recognize God's Word addressed to him. He paid no attention to what God was saying to him through this poor man. He let the poor man eat crumbs from his table, and he never felt responsible for him. No need for him to kill him; it was enough to harden his heart against God's question. We know how the story turns out, and that sheds light on the meaning of this responsibility.

For when we thus challenge God's question, we stop being responsible. We stop being the head and king of creation. We completely stop being the image of God. We stop being human. Whatever our attitude, there is no way out. If we agree to respond, we are condemned by the existence of the poor; if we refuse to respond, we are condemned by our very refusal. Such is our situation, a dilemma from which we can be extricated only by grace, once we have taken it seriously and agreed to stake our whole life on it.

This cruel fact, which leaves us no way of escape, was clearly understood by the disciples. When Jesus said to them, "It is easier for a camel to go through the eye of a needle than for a rich man to enter the kingdom of God," they gave this shocking response: "Who then can be saved?" (Mt 19:24-25). It is the disciples who are saying this, men who have left everything—fortune, family, chance for advancement—to follow Jesus Christ, who also are poor along with the Poor One. And yet these men recognize that they are among the rich, among the unsaved, because they know the impassable distance that still remains between them and the Poor One. How then could we not recognize ourselves among the rich?

Jesus answers them simply by affirming omnipotent grace.

Responding to the Poor. Nevertheless many think the situation is not that dramatic. Are there not many ways to respond to the poor with kindness and good will? But this is not exactly the problem. The condition of the poor, we could even say their nature, is not there to arouse our interest or our charity (in the modern sense of the term).

This is no place for pity. Human pity can offer the poor only appeasement, falsehoods and loss of consciousness. What realistic bitterness we find in Lemuel's words when he says, "Give strong drink to him who is perishing, and wine to those in bitter distress; let them drink and forget their poverty, and remember their misery no more" (Prov 31:6-7). This is all a person of good will can do for the poor; for the reality of human misery, the negative reflection of money's power, goes infinitely beyond human capacities. And in one form or another, it is always the same diversion and oblivion and loss of consciousness that is proposed to the poor, in hatred or in love, in religion or communism or comfort. It is the same falsehood, and we cannot accept it.

Giving money to the poor does not in any way change our relation to them. This is why Jesus reprimands his disciples when they wish they had the money that was wasted on perfume and that would have been better given to the poor. The disciples are wrong to contrast this wasted money with money for the poor. For money is not what will change the situation of the poor. Paul reminds us of the same truth: "And though I bestow all my goods to feed the poor, . . . and have not love, it profiteth me nothing" (1 Cor 13:3 KJV).

Of course, we must underline the *me*. Giving money to a poor person will obviously profit the poor person. But we have a totally erroneous idea of evangelical teaching if we think that everything stops there, if we think that all we have to do is relieve misery. No, for as we do that, we are in the position of the rich who pity the poor—yet who, in the long run, stay rich. Even their solicitude is not good for the poor, for the relation between them is always as described in Scripture.

But does this mean that there is nothing we can do? Our disinclination is reinforced by the idea that if the poor are truly the image of Jesus Christ, then they must be quite happy, so why help them? These are temptations: the temptation to run away from our responsibility and, more serious, the temptation to take the place of Jesus Christ. For only Jesus can say, "Blessed are you poor" (Lk 6:20). We do not have the right to say that to the poor. To Jesus alone belong the blessing and the curse; the church must not try to take his place.

Of course we must do everything possible to relieve misfortune, approaching the poor as if we were speaking to Jesus Christ himself. Here the situation is strangely reversed. For do we approach Christ as if we were rich? Yes, of course, for we crucified him; that is, in his presence we certainly did take the attitude of the rich. But when we proceed like that, we well know what awaits us. Thus we can no longer deny our responsibility. In approaching the poor, we are required to get rid of the easy conscience of the rich. This is especially true if we see the poor as God's personal question in our lives. Then the existence of misfortune becomes intolerable to us, and we will agree to do anything, to risk everything, to involve ourselves totally so that the situation of the poor can be changed.

But if their condition can change, does that mean we should work to turn the poor into the rich—and in so doing, cause them to pass from those who are pronounced "Blessed" to those who are warned "Woe to you, rich . . ."? For it never takes much for the poor to become rich. Once again, this is not the response asked of us. If, by extraordinary luck, we managed to get rid of all misfortune, to make everyone rich (first economically, then spiritually), then this "Woe to you" would ring out for everyone. Then we would pay for this universal happiness based on Mammon worship. There is no other possibility.

In this emergency, how should we offer the help that Christ's compassion requires? All we can do, like what Christ himself did, is a prophetic sign of the coming kingdom. It is to bring hope and grace in material form to the poor who are indeed under the Lord's blessing.

Here we find ourselves in direct opposition to Marxism. But the ideal is not always a synthesis which unavoidably emasculates Christianity.

This opposition to Marxism is even more obvious when we consider that the Bible requires personal involvement. The question raised by the poor is not sociological but individual.

It is not an economic question either. The only place in the Bible where a person thinks that the problem of the poor is *first of all* a question of the distribution of money, and thus an economic question, is in the example given by Judas. For Judas the important thing is to give money to the poor. It is to settle the economic question. But he thinks this way precisely because he is Judas. And his attitude leads him with relentless logic to sell the Poor One. This judgment and this perspective are just as valid today. All who wish to see only the economic problem and restrict the poor to their lack of money are ultimately the Judases of the poor, and are led sooner or later to sell the poor to the powerful, as we observe in the Communist party.

The Need for Personal Involvement. We do not have to respond with a sociological attitude or an economic system but by personal involvement.

Here, as in many other areas, Christianity rejects the system. The proper response to the poor will not be found in adherence to any group or program. To try to respond by joining a party, by accepting a program, by working at an institution, is to refuse responsibility, to escape into the crowds when confronted with God's question. The solutions that we think are a response, whether social, economic or otherwise, are a dangerous lie. They are a way of getting rid of a troubling personal situation.

They are a way of turning over to the group, to others, to the collectivity, our own personal burden. "I'm not the one who's responsible. It's the owner, the communist, the fascist who is guilty. And it is the party, technology, the government who are responsible for putting things right. No doubt I will help out in this work. But I take nothing on myself. And I do so many things that I have done my duty toward the poor—I don't need to know any of them because I work with others to change their situation."

This is also a way of turning over to the future what is a question for the present. For we talk of moving toward a time (quite distant!) when there will be no more poor. We can forget the poor of today or even make them die a bit more quickly—today's holocaust will assure better times to their great-great-grandchildren. Once again, it is a cheap way to avoid God's question. We find again here, at the end of this long search, the ideas we put forth at the beginning.

The only attitude that Christianity can require is personal commitment. We must take personal responsibility for the state of the poor; this is being responsible before God. But we are entering dangerous territory. We must not sweeten the gospel to make it acceptable. All we can do is measure our faith against the Word spoken to us, God's question which puts our life in question. To accept our responsibility is to enter into the spiritual and material condition of those who put God's question to the world. It is, in fact, to become poor ourselves with the poor, with the Poor One.

This is Jesus' very attitude, joined to our own. Paul reminds us: "Let each of you look not only to his own interests, but also to the interests of others. Have this mind among yourselves, which is yours in Christ Jesus, who ... emptied himself, ... humbled himself" (Phil 2:4-8). Jesus' attitude conditions our own.

In the Protestant Church we have too often given up the imitation of Christ (one of the essential elements of the Christian life), forgetting that salvation by grace does not conflict with this imitation. James says to us, "Let the rich man glory in his humiliation, because like flowering grass he will pass away. For the sun rises with a scorching wind, and withers the grass; and its flower falls off, and the beauty of its appearance is destroyed; so too the rich man in the midst of his pursuits will fade away" (Jas 1:10-11 NASB). We are told here that in the presence of the Lord's grace and glory, the rich are stripped of their riches, exactly like the grass is stripped of its flowers by the drought. The first result of this encounter is thus the withering of the power of the rich, of their enterprises. They are humiliated. As long as they are not humiliated, we cannot be sure that this encounter has happened. The humiliation of the rich is the loss of their wealth. And all that the rich can justifiably boast of before God is to have been stripped of their riches, to have become one of the poor. They can boast of this, for this is participation in the very glory of Jesus Christ.

All this is just the theoretical formulation of the story of the meeting between Jesus and the rich young man (Mt 19:16-22). There also the question of the poor is asked in Christ. Admirably, this question is also a response to anguish, to the human drama. The rich young man asks a question, and in response God makes him confront his responsibility before God's own question.

We see in this story everything we have described up to this point: material emptying ("sell what you possess"), spiritual emptying ("follow me"), joining the ranks of the poor without there being any social solution, without any amelioration of their fate ("give to the poor").

We must not be confused: the subject here is not salvation. Salvation is entrusted to God's grace, and nowhere are we told that this rich young man is lost; in fact, the implication is quite otherwise. The subject is our attitude, our life, our response to God's question about our actions and our concept of life. Here and nowhere else we are at the heart of the whole problem of ethics. The story itself tells us this: "If you would be perfect," Jesus says to the rich young man.

Meditation

In front of the manger where God's gift lies, the shepherds have come to worship, as we have ourselves. Shepherds, poorest of the poor— these are servants, half slaves, having nothing of their own, working for others, watching the flocks of others in the fields by night.

And the Magi, richest of the rich. We call them magician-kings, and this is not far from the truth. In their Eastern country they are primarily scientists and priests, clever in their understanding of stars, of mathematics, of administration. And little by little, because their knowledge was respected, they became wealthy, and political power depended largely on their decisions. Magician-kings, rich in intelligence, in money, in power. The poor and the rich, equally called to worship before the one who is already a sign of contradiction, the King of kings in the straw. King of these powerful Magi, and poor with the very poverty of these shepherds.

All have been equally called, each in the language that suited him, that spoke to his heart and his intelligence. Each in his own tongue, as later, when the Lord established his church, each heard in his own tongue about the mighty works of God.

These poor men believe in legends, in fairies, in the supernatural, in miracles. At the same time, they are sensitive to spiritual realities. They know what prayer is and they are waiting for deliverance. They know what meditation is (as all shepherds do) and are directly open to revelation. Thus God speaks to them in their own tongue, by miracle and revelation: the angels descend and call them. He gives them the sign which both satisfies and reassures them, which is within their reach: a baby in a sheep pen.

These rich men probably do not believe in angels. But they believe in their science; they know how to interpret signs in the heavens; they want to explain what seems abnormal. Thus God speaks to them in their tongue by means of the star, an incomprehensible sign. But it is impossible for them to accept that it is incomprehensible, for this would disparage the laws they know well, laws of science and of destiny. God calls them in their intelligence. He gives them a political sign, which also speaks to their concerns. Politically minded as they are, they know that King Herod's hatred for the baby is a struggle for power.

Rich and poor, equally called.

But the poor are called first. In the kingdom of heaven, the first in this world are the last to arrive. The shepherds arrive first. So close to God's heart because of their poverty, they were right there, near the sheep pen, which is their own place. Jesus entered human misery, and those who live in misery find him only a few steps away. This does not mean that the poor are better, or that they can boast of being poor (when they do that, they become rich!). It means only that Jesus came where they are. And the revelation given to them is direct and immediate. It reaches them at the center of their lives. As soon as they believed, we find them at the door of the sheepfold.

The rich are next. They have a long road to travel. Wise men from the East, they went on a long journey. They crossed the deserts: deserts of the vanity of riches, of money, of power. They followed a difficult road with countless obstacles to overcome, some of which seemed beyond human strength ("Go, sell what you possess.... And ... the young man went away sorrowful; for he had great possessions"). They had to be patient with themselves, but demanding. They had to turn their thirst for knowledge in one direction alone, to use all the resources of their understanding and their wealth (for such an expedition is expensive!). This does not mean that they were more meritorious than those who had only a few steps to take. They were farther away because they had excellent human advantages. They learned little by little that these excellent advantages separated them from God. And since the call passed over these barriers to reach them, they also had to go through obstacles to reach him.

Rich and poor alike called to worship, each with what he could bring.

The shepherds, in their worship, brought themselves. For they had nothing else. They came with nothing in their hands, but they brought their prayer, their song, their lives. They glorified and praised God, and when they left they became the first witnesses of Jesus; they told what they had seen and heard, and all who heard them were amazed at the good news. The first witnesses, the first evangelists: this is their gift of themselves and their worship.

The Magi, in their worship, brought something that in their eyes was worth more than themselves. Gold, the symbol of their wealth and also of all the wealth in the world. Incense, with which kings are honored, symbol of political power. Myrrh, used for embalming, symbol of the Magi's mysterious powers, perhaps of science. Bringing these gifts, the Magi put into God's hands the very powers of this world. They recognized that these powers belong to this baby. These rich men, having given up their attachment to riches, had to come so that man could offer his Lord everything that gives him earthly power. The poor could not offer what they did not have, but the rich could pay tribute with the world's wealth.

And this was not a purely spiritual tribute, for when these kings went away, they no longer had their gold, incense and myrrh. They left these things in the hands of the Lord. They gave themselves along with their most precious possessions, for, when they went away, they also became witnesses—protectors of the small child that King Herod wanted to sacrifice. These magician-kings broke with political solidarity. On the way in, they had of course agreed to meet King Herod. Power met with power. They had mutual interests. But on their way out, they were on Jesus' side and betrayed their own interests. They no longer obeyed Herod and hid from him what they now knew about the true King of the world.

Poor and rich, equally witnesses because equally called. They were called *first,* before they did a thing, and their situation is the same. Each does his own work. The shepherds watch sheep; the Magi study. They are not interested in God. God is interested in them and calls them. He calls them to worship, to offer up what is dearest to them, because God gives them, first of all, what is dearest to him: his Son.

For the rich and for the poor, Christmas worship is self-emptying worship because God on Christmas night emptied himself. He took the initiative and gave up his power, his eternity, himself, to come to this place where we could finally see him.

AFTERWORD [1979]

SINCE 1950 WHEN THIS BOOK WAS WRITTEN, MUCH HAS CHANGED IN appearance, very little in reality. Tendencies toward the growth of the power of money have increased; theological reflection on the poor has expanded. These are the two points that I would like quickly to mention.

The power of money? After all it is not more aggressive today than in the nineteenth century. To be sure, we have passed from a period of capitalism to a period of imperialism, from a society of production to a society of consumption. But today like yesterday, everything is sold, everything is bought . . . probably no more so now than then. Nevertheless, I think it will be helpful briefly to recall three facts.

First, in the area of institutions, the phenomenon of the multinational corporations. The big manufacturing firms are no longer content to invade the world market to sell their products or to establish sales outlets everywhere. Now distribution takes place on a level with production, under the form of production subsidiaries established in all countries. Thus we pass to a new economic structure. It is now directed, no longer by commercial gain, but entirely by industrial profit. We pass from an international economy, with each firm located within the borders of a country and conducting business abroad, to a world economy, economic production networks having practically annulled national division.

These huge multinational firms draw the most diverse countries into their orbit. For the system operates not only for the poor countries of the Third World, but also for Europe in connection with American and Japanese firms. Moreover, it is obvious that these multinationals cannot be really endangered by political change: if one tentacle is cut, the animal is still whole and will grow another one. What is most interesting is that the socialist countries also are ready to jump into the game. Markets between China and Japan, the opening of China to the installation of factories from France or Germany, "keys in hand," show the obvious possibility of multinational expansion (camouflaged) toward China. This is one aspect of this growth of the power of money.

I also want to point out a transformation in today's better understanding of the idea of merchandise. We know that this idea of merchandise is central to Marx, but it has been somewhat played down since then. Since 1968, however, it appears that a certain rereading of Marx is restoring merchandise to its place in understanding society. It is not uniquely the capitalist structure, but really the power of money itself, that reduces everything to merchandise. Indeed, not only is everything bought and sold, but everything is done *with the intention* of buying and selling. All actions and transactions can be explained by the fact that everything has been turned into merchandise. In addition, value is defined as market value, and the first thing we think about in any area is merchandise. It is the reality of merchandise that gives our society its character. Nothing escapes this predominance. We know that Marx showed that the modern world's inhuman character is tied to the status of merchandise, and that we can understand human relations (distorted, perverted, degraded) only insofar as we understand that everything has become merchandise in these relations.

But the law of merchandise exists wherever money exists. It does not result only from bad use, or from a particular economic structure: money is implicated by its nature. The only problem is to know if money is dominant or not, that is, if individuals and structures give free rein to the power of money and its law. The necessary connection between money and merchandise, as well as the specific characteristics of merchandise, has been more deeply studied and better understood in the last ten years. This awareness seems to me to be fundamental and positive; but awareness, alas, is not enough to shake the power of money.

If we can thus point out a positive development, by contrast we must mention a negative fact in a most important area. In the last twenty years we have seen indisputable efforts to break the power of money. They have all failed. I will mention only Cuba and China. Even with the local differences and peculiarities based on the size and economic complexity of their countries, the principle was still the same. The two countries attempted the same three things.

First, they got rid of money as a means of exchange, replacing money value with consumer coupons. Second, they made it impossible to save money, to lay it aside, to build up capital. Reserves were neither useful nor desirable because needs were to be covered as they were experienced and, of course, as goods were produced to satisfy them. Because of these first two measures, goods obviously stopped being merchandise. They were produced with direct consumption in mind and were not the object of successive exchanges.

The third measure led to numerous discussions. It has been called the "moral or ideological stimulus." I mention only this: the worker must produce and work because he believes in the usefulness of his work, because he wants to build communism, because he is well-trained ideologically—never for profit or personal advantage. The fact that a worker may have particularly high productivity, that he may devote himself eagerly to his work, must not be translated into supplementary gain, which would introduce inequality. Reciprocally, no production bonuses must be proposed to make people work better and more, for that would be to follow the lure of gain, which would go against the socialist conscience, since bonuses and supplementary pay are seen as an aspect of a money economy. The true, good communist works for nothing but honor, and his sole recompense is to be held up as a model to his comrades.

We must note moreover that these three antimoney orientations were already affirmed in the USSR in 1918. But progressively in Cuba and China, as in the USSR forty or fifty years earlier, these imperatives had to be abandoned. Money as means of exchange, then money as means of saving, reappeared. Finally it had to be recognized that the ideological stimulus had failed completely, and cash production bonuses were brought back.

After reestablishing money in all its functions, Cuba set up a small-scale model of exemplary communist society on the Isle of Pines in about 1970. But after several promising news releases, fog closed in around this experiment. As for China, nothing is left of its former condemnation of money. I am not writing this as an attack against Communist regimes (I am convinced that in these countries the experiment was carried out as well as possible); I am only pointing out the incredible power of money, which survives every trial, every upset, as if a merchant mentality has so permeated the world's consciousness that there is no longer any possibility of going against it. And as was seen in the USSR, as soon as money is reinstated, *all* its consequences that we know in a capitalist regime reappear (for example, the amazing possibility in the USSR to lend money at interest). What we have just briefly mentioned confirms in real life what we have already said about the strange, bewitching, independent power of something that should never have been more than a neutral instrument.

Contemporary Theological Discussions of the Poor

But another feature that seems characteristic of this thirty-year period is the fact that, in Western Christian circles, the theme of the poor has become a cliché in religious and even theological writings. We can no longer open a book or skim an article without running into the theme song with its quavering notes about the humble and the oppressed; it seems that our religious authors are no longer capable of any other reflection. Whether it has to do with the faith or God or salvation or incarnation or eschatology or the kingdom, the poor are now the key to everything, the explanation, the reference, the common ground.

And of course this cohort of authors in their impetuous youth think they are saying something which at last is new and authentic in opposition to the horrible theology of power. Up to their time, the church has always been mistaken. It has always seen God as a barbarian King and Christ as a stifling almighty ruler. Fortunately, since 1968 these theologians have been reestablishing the truth about the poor Jesus after twenty centuries of error. I exaggerate only a little.[1]

These people are simply forgetting that reflection on Christ's self-emptying, on his identity with the poor, on the poor (the leprous) as image of Christ are centers of patristic thought, especially that of the desert fathers. It is also the central thought of the whole medieval

---

[1]As one example among a thousand, take the following text, which shall remain anonymous: "For a long time men have thought that they were building the kingdom proclaimed by Christ: they trusted in the desire for power and truth which stirred their hearts, and they understood this to fulfill righteousness. But who has seen God in the intelligence of the clever, the triumph of the strong, or even the unremembered happiness of the multitudes? He is no longer in these things, if ever he was. When I look at man and the works of his reason, and this formidable task undertaken in the world, I do not discover Jesus. When I look at the earth torn with injustice and blind wilfullness, I do not find the trace of a god, and religions which lack power or act as accomplices should be rejected.

"Now, suddenly, God rises up in the only place where he should have been sought: in the suffering of the humble. How can I think of him without having the faces of these beggars, these captives, these starving men, these despised ones, these unwanted children, these men and these women whom nobody has invited to life's banquet, pass before my eyes? *Their anguish is God.*"

period. The poor are the true representatives of God on earth. This emphasis fades away during the Reformation (and this is one of the complaints of many Catholic thinkers against the Reformation: Leon Bloy, for example) and tends to disappear with the rise of the middle class. But it takes humility to put oneself under the tutelage of the Middle Ages rather than to pride oneself on having such a lovely hermeneutic.

Nevertheless, today's discussion of the poor has two new characteristics. First there has been a major shift from classical theology (called to mind in my essay) in which Jesus emptied himself of his divinity, of his power, of his grandeur and chose to become the Poor One. It is because of this choice, this decision, that the poor have become Christ's image. They have no dignity or value by themselves; it is not poverty which reveals God or sanctifies man. It is because Jesus stands behind them that the poor, in calling forth our love, are for us a sign of God's love. The poor are a sign pointing to someone bigger than they are, even if Jesus identified himself with the poor ("you did it to me"). Nevertheless, the poor still are nothing by themselves. Jesus has not melted away and disappeared; he is the one who gives the poor their significance and their radical importance.

But from this starting point we have gone on to a more complete identification. Jesus is *nothing but* the poor, and each poor person is by himself the presence of Christ (presence, and not reference or sign). The poor become a sort of sacrament. There is basically no other gospel message but poverty. A step further: the poor are revealers par excellence. Since we know God only through Jesus, in the modern temptation God disappears (or does not interest us further) and leaves only his image. We look at Jesus only in his humanity. But we do not know this Jesus himself; the Gospels are dubious witnesses. At least we know one thing for sure—he identified himself with the poor. Consequently, the poor become the only representation we can have or make of Jesus.

Now that we have stopped scrutinizing the heavens to find a hidden God, let us stop scrutinizing the Bible to find an equally hidden Jesus:

we have in our midst all that is necessary. Any poor person is, in himself and by himself, Jesus. Let us contemplate this poor person, and we have all there is to have of Jesus. And from this we proceed a step lower. There is no need to appeal to a third party to give value to the poor person. It is unnecessary to imagine some sort of transcendent Jesus. The poor person is sufficient unto himself; by himself he is God's revelation.

This also provides one of the modernist interpretations of the resurrection (all of which try to avoid the question of the new life of the body!); Jesus' resurrection is the fact that he is himself present in all poor people. There is no need to think of a glorified body coming out of the tomb, for Jesus says, "You did it to me." Therefore he is fully present in the poor; his resurrection is the poor, here and now. Of course, all this in reality results from great laxity of thought, from concern for good style and literary effects, but this lack of awareness is itself quite illuminating.

The second great transformation of the theology of the poor is political. In spite of textual distortions, it is impossible to say that Jesus was involved in politics, that he sided with a class and fomented a revolution on behalf of the oppressed. He did not meet with and speak about the poor as a social or economic category, as a group; it is always individuals, specific poor people, that he singles out and approaches. He did not found the party of the poor. He did not instigate their revolution: he always responded to their expectations in another way. To the poor man who asked for money, Peter answers, "I have no silver and gold, but I give you what I have."

This is Jesus' kind of answer. But our modern theologians are above all imbued with the sociopolitical ideas of the age, and because in the nineteenth century socialists alone sided with and defended the proletariat (not all the poor—poor peasants hardly interested them), these Christian intellectuals are therefore, with the necessary lapse of time, imbued with socialism.

This has two major results for the theology of the poor. The first is that the poor are looked at from an economic point of view exclusively. The poor are those who have no money, who are exploited in their work and deprived of the fruit of their labors. When modern theologians speak of the humble, they speak in terms of financial poverty. This goes directly against the biblical image of the poor, as we have shown. Jesus spends time with rich men (publicans) who are poor (misjudged and scorned) socially. He spends time with Roman officers who are poor because they are sorrowful. All this is forgotten in order to keep nothing but "deprivation of economic means."

Collectivization is the second result of modern theology's adoption of sociopolitical ideas. It is no longer the poor individual but the poor class that is important. Similarly, I am not told to respond to the direct, immediate, personal need of the poor person I meet, but to go back to the "causes," that is, to the economic and political regime which produced this situation. The gospel proclaimed to the poor is that they are politically liberated from class distinctions. Of course it is easy to condemn harshly the private charity which is an alibi for covering and tolerating social injustice. It is easy to rail about the fact that we love in words and not in deeds. This is all accurate. But does this mean that we have to go over to the class struggle, the desire to destroy the root of poverty by political means?

In any case we must note that by this globalization we totally lost contact with the poor that we know personally. We work in the abstract toward the liberation of a social category that we never meet. We know the political leaders of this class, who are no longer poor themselves. And this globalization, this depersonalization of the poor, surely means that a person who is poor simply because he is sick or is mourning the loss of a loved one or has been humiliated by a failure in life arouses no interest if he belongs to the exploiting class.

We must realize that all this is the result of political ideology and not of the gospel, and theologically it is the end of a long chain of reasoning. We go from the poor individual to the poor, to the poor as a group, to the poor class, to the regime which makes them a class, to the exploitation on which this regime is built, to the evil of this exploitation because the poor are good, to the fight against this regime, to politics or revolution. . . . But this is exactly the type of reasoning which from the beginnings of Christianity has led theologians to extract from the biblical text judgments and behaviors that, outside their social context and a century or two later, look like monstrosities. We can no longer begin to imagine how Christians could have come to such conclusions.

At the origin of the Inquisition, of Constantinianism, of the Crusades, of Cesaropapism, of the idea of money as a blessing, there has always been a just, biblical and true starting point. But the multiplicity of arguments leading us further and further from the text, producing a construction that matches the ideology of the age (and that therefore looks obvious in that milieu), leads to appalling perversions, emanating from the Prince of Lies. Today, starting with the profound, fundamental gospel truth about the poor, we are watching the same perversion, the same slap in the face of Christ. For the poor, who think they are being liberated, are each time thrown in to a slavery that is worse than the former one.